GOLD Counselling™

A Practical Psychology

with

NLP

By

Georges Philips
&
Lyn Buncher

with Brian Stevenson

Published by The Anglo American Book Company,
Bancyfelin, Carmarthen, Wales.

First published in the UK by

The Anglo American Book Company Ltd
Crown Buildings
Bancyfelin
Carmarthen
Wales

First published 1997.

British Library of Cataloguing-in-Publication Data
A catalogue entry for this book is available
from the British Library.

ISBN 1899836063

Printed and bound by Antony Rowe Ltd.,
Bumper's Farm, Chippenham, Wiltshire.

June 1998

To: Bendy

" One must have chaos in one's life
to give birth to a dancing star."
                              NIETZSCHE.

Thanks for fixing the ear.
                George + Lyndy

We dedicate this book to the spirit of life
which we know is within all of you

How to understand how your beliefs underpin
EVERY action you've EVER carried out and EVERY
feeling you've ever had ... and how to revise those beliefs so as to
create your own successes.

Techniques to deal with "lies, damned lies, and beliefs".

How to understand why so many techniques that you may have
tried before, did not work and would not ever have worked, permanently.

An advanced therapists' guidebook to applying
GOLD Counselling™ analysis procedures with NLP
to facilitate change in clients' lives, and in your own,
permanently.

Acknowledgments

This book would not have been possible without the pioneering work of Steve and Connirae Andreas, Richard Bandler, Robert Dilts, John Grinder and other major developers of NLP. Also Edward De Bono, Deepak Chopra and Stuart Wild who have influenced the making of this book through their work on personal development.

Our thanks

... Many thanks to the many people whom we've worked with and who have made this book possible ... lots of people ... too numerous to mention ... but with special thanks to Peter Crawford, Lyne Driscoll, Susan Ermelli, Michelle Harris, Tina Hawkins, Jacquelyne Morison, Andy Parr, and Vera Peiffer, to name but a few.

Table of Contents

Foreword
by Dr Sheila Cromwell

It is a pleasure to read a thesis set out with such clarity, and to follow through the lucid development. The NLP field is an accretion of many ideas and strategies from different sources. Strength and interest is derived from these successive inputs. It would be a pity if rigid fossilisation should ever set in. There is always room for fresh thought.

It is therefore refreshing to discover a new system slotted in. Not that the authors claim that the system they have developed is an NLP technique. However, a time-honoured NLP pattern is apparent in that Primary Beliefs are intuitively accessed in a light trance state and then cognitively questioned, albeit within limits. This mixture of intuition and cognition, while characteristically 'NLP' in concept, has been developed by the authors in "Gold Counselling" in a system all their own - a system that stands sturdily on its own. By repetitive gentle questioning on a theme (with verbal variation), negative Primary Beliefs are deconstructed.

It can be said that NLP has been slotted into this process. NLP practitioners, well-versed in the ecological implications of the NLP strategies referred to in the final section, will find a useful additional tool, and one that can be used more broadly even than has been indicated.

I particularly liked the freshness of thought that questioned time-honoured concepts and presuppositions, as in 'planning to fail' (page 199) and in the authors' Structural Pre-suppositions I and 2 on page 62.

The possible conflict of beliefs is thoughtfully approached and the dangers of seeking integration before resolution of the differences are indicated, (in a parallel way, but through a totally different strategy, to that of Robert Dilts et. al. who warned of an otherwise possible disintegration of a client's thinking process, in *Beliefs*, Metamorphous Press 1990).

The outstanding merit of this book lies in the mapping. Once the client has, through a process of free-thinking in a light trance, made a list of words associated (however seemingly remotely and loosely) with the therapy topic, then, by means of mapping their connections, the client's primary beliefs with regard to that topic are derived. These maps, generously illustrated, are helpfully clear.

I think this book is a very useful addition to therapeutic practice and deserves the success I wish it.

Sheila Cromwell

*Have you ever wondered what you could
achieve if you believed, yes you really believed,
you could **ONLY** succeed? ......*

... so WHY aren't you doing it, right now?

Preface

Everything that we ever say or do starts from an idea which we think.

How often have you heard people say things like, *"you can't teach an old dog new tricks"*, or perhaps, *"No, I can't do that. Tried it once and failed."* Another regularly used phrase is *"But what if I fail?"*

Well, if these phrases ring any bells with you you're not alone. We have used these words too. Even now in the latter part of the twentieth century with all the possibilities we have around us, why is it that so many people live lives that are but a pale imitation of the lives which they could really live? It's just that they don't believe that they could achieve that which they want.

During the last few years, significant advances have been made in the understandings of how we think and operate within the world. From these advances, it has been possible to develop a new way of thinking to become aware of the ideas, values and beliefs which are stored within each of us.

By integrating these new understandings, it has been possible to create an approach which permits us to effectively "see inside" another person's mind and to remove any of the limitations which are stored in there. The techniques which we have developed to enable this to take place are known as GOLD Counselling™. This approach is, quite simply, the most powerful, most efficient and most effective way to restructure beliefs yet devised.

At this point a word of caution is called for. As you continue to read further into this book, you will find certain comments which may appear impossible or perhaps implausible. Yes, some do sound strange. Yes, some do feel impossible. Yes, some appear to go against considered wisdom. And, yes, they are all true.

Once you have grasped the essence of what GOLD Counselling™ is, you will understand more about the unconscious mind than most therapists of whatever school anywhere in the world. We know the techniques work. We understand why they work. And we can prove they work. We have found them to facilitate **permanent** success with our clients, time and time again.

Many of you reading this book will already be either competent in Neuro-Linguistic Programming (NLP), or undergoing training in that field. We have found that the skills available to NLP Practitioners at whatever level are significant life-enhancing tools. However, these tools do not as yet integrate the specific new learnings which have been identified. It is by applying these new learnings which you will find presented in this book that you will be able to truly understand, possibly for the very first time, why so many people fail to achieve those things which they believe they really want in life.

How this book is structured

Within Section One of this book we have set out an explanation of how the mind operates using its beliefs, and how each of these beliefs connects to other beliefs, be they liberating or restricting. We then explain exactly how permanent and self-perpetuating these beliefs are. Once installed, whatever that person does will always be filtered through these beliefs on an unconscious level.

You will learn and find explanations as to how the mind uses energy to fulfil beliefs, why it is that we all seem to hold apparently conflicting beliefs and how it is possible to experience such things as elation one minute and depression the next.

Section Two of this book contains the key elements which you must understand so that you can appreciate what GOLD Counselling™ is and how it works. The first chapter in Section Two gives an explanation of why positive thinking is not able to create change on a permanent basis. You will find an explanation of how this method of counselling can be applied to identify and eliminate limiting beliefs. Once this elimination has taken place, a person will then be able to naturally and effortlessly take himself forward towards the success which he desires in a congruent and focused manner.

Throughout this Section we have incorporated examples to highlight and focus awareness on the specific issues being raised. Actual case studies are included which elaborate further the process of GOLD Counselling™. By reference to these examples, we would expect a therapist to gain a deeper understanding of how this process works and realise the speed, power and accuracy of the techniques within this book.

Section Three contains actual client case studies. This section is structured so that the examples become progressively more complex and involved, showing you the breadth of presenting problems which can be effectively worked through with these techniques.

Finally, Section Four is structured so that people with a working knowl-edge of NLP will be able to appreciate how the GOLD Counselling™ approach can be used in conjunction with specific NLP techniques. Each chapter contains context-specific examples in order to identify how these would occur in a therapeutic situation. The NLP techniques discussed include such procedures as swish, six-step reframes, new-behaviour generators and well-formed outcomes.

When you study this section you will realise that at all times we thoroughly endorse the existing NLP techniques. Where we find a synergetic overlap is in using the GOLD Counselling™ approach in order to identify and work through the underlying cause, rather than just working with the symptom. Once carried out, if additional techniques are required these can then be applied to the correct place in the client's map of experiences.

If you are an NLP Practitioner of whatever level, beginner, intermediate or advanced, GOLD Counselling™ will expose you to the possibility of so many more successes than you could have ever imagined before.

We have taught these techniques to NLP Practitioners who have then gone on to significantly improve the quality of their work.

Section One:

How The Mind Works

Introduction to Section One

Within this section we have set out how the mind operates and explained how the two separate parts, the conscious mind and the unconscious mind, relate to each other. You will find an explanation of the way in which memory, energy and words are used within the mind and how the unconscious mind sorts and categorises every belief you have ever held.

1. A Metaphor For The Mind

It has been said that however well someone is trained to drive a car or ride a motorbike, one of the greatest ways of differentiating one person's competency from another is to notice how much feel they have for the machine they are operating. Perhaps you've been in a car with someone who habitually revs the engine up to the maximum every time before changing up a gear, someone who accelerates hard towards the red light ahead and, at the last minute, slams on the breaks.

Or perhaps, going to the other extreme, someone who is over-cautious, so timid and unwilling to use the power within the machine that he actually seems to create that accident which he fears so much. Whereas if someone, while learning how to drive a car or ride a motorbike, is also taught how the actual machinery works, then he would have a better feel for it and would be that much more able to stay in control. This shows up in situations when unexpected occurrences take place, such as driving over a patch of black ice and then loosing control of the direction of travel.

In the same way, we all have within us a brain of awesome power and potential, but no training was ever given or any user's manual supplied.

This wouldn't be so bad if, like those engines in the cars and motorbikes, we could take our brains apart and look inside to understand how it all works, but, unfortunately, it's not as simple as that. Notwithstanding all the scientific research which has been applied to the brain and its thinking patterns, no-one can explain scientifically how it actually works.

Furthermore, whenever we are unhappy with life or feel disease (spelt *dis-ease*), or infection (spelt *in-fection*), we are experiencing the anomalies that we create between what we believe to be true and what is true. Since the only reference point within our unconscious mind is what the unconscious mind believes to be real. Whenever we feel good or bad or indifferent about an incident, it must be because of the way thoughts have been stored and coded within our mind. And this thought has, in turn, led to the creation of a belief about the world or life or a particular facet thereof.

To elaborate further, consider the following. Medical research has proven that if one group of patients is given a specific drug to speed up their heartbeat, a second group given a drug to slow their heartbeat and a third group administered a placebo, a neutral-effect substance, then the following is known to occur: Whatever the patients are told will be caused by the drug *will* occur within them. If the people given the placebo are told that they will find their heartbeat increasing and they believe it, then it will happen. And if people are given a drug to increase their heartbeat, but advised that the drug will slow it down, then, if they believe it, their heartbeat will actually slow down.

2. *What Are Thoughts And Beliefs?*

2.1 Where do beliefs originate?

Let us assume for a moment that a client visits you to gain assistance in increasing his confidence. If you were to start the process by asking him about what may be stopping him from having confidence, he would probably respond with comments about feelings of or memories of past lapses in confidence or such like. Perhaps in some cases he would not be able to be so specific. It may be just a general feeling which he has that stops him.

If he did have any memories to explain why he was not confident, then each of these individual thoughts will have become justifying reasons why he believes this is so. These explanations could take the shape of many different thoughts and memories. Perhaps he was bullied at school, perhaps he didn't feel he had any role models, or perhaps he may have confused confidence with aggression, or perhaps he doesn't feel he deserves the things confidence will bring, and so on. Each of these thoughts must have originated at a certain time in his life and will have been generated from a wide variety of sources.

All of these thoughts combine together to create a belief which has been formed by that person's experience. As therapists in the present we don't know, and possibly may never know, whether that person's experience was real or imagined, or whether his interpretation was true or false. However, we can be certain that on that particular day, at that particular time in the past, that person interpreted his thoughts in a certain way and from those thoughts a belief was created. A belief as to what that thought meant to him.

Once an interpretation, or belief has been given to a thought, it then becomes a reference point to enable that person to understand the world and, at the same time, it becomes part of a structure that the unconscious mind will use to filter and sort all subsequent thoughts.

Naturally, this method of using beliefs to filter and sort new thoughts will create more thoughts of a similar belief. Take, for example, the injunction *"Don't think of pink elephants."* How many of you, when filtering your minds with that injunction would be able to see nothing except pink elephants? Beliefs, in simple terms, operate in a similar way.

2.2 Beliefs are created from thoughts

If we reconsider the client without confidence, given enough time you could continue to ask the question "Why?" to this person until you had identified all the different thoughts which he holds which are in turn the reasons why he considers himself to be without confidence. However, the actual list of thoughts could run into hundreds if the issue were very profound and important to him.

As you continue to read this book you will learn techniques to enable you to focus your client's unconscious mind so that a simplified list of the main thoughts which comprise your client's beliefs can be formed in a very short time.

It is from these individual thoughts that a belief about something is formed. Once formed, other thoughts will attach themselves to one or more of the existing beliefs within the unconscious mind and serve to reinforce the original belief.

Compare this for a moment with a game of patience. Consider how, when playing a game of patience, once the initial base cards have been dealt (equivalent to a child's first thoughts and beliefs), all other cards are required to be played in a manner which connects with those already laid down. These are the rules of the game, only certain moves (or connections) are valid in the game (equivalent to the unconscious mind).

Within the unconscious mind, a thought will never be free-floating on its own, it will always attach itself to another thought. The unconscious mind will sift and sort through all the thoughts that we have and then collate these in certain ways, often with one thought having more than one other thought connecting to it.

I am sure that most people reading this book will have at some stage in their lives looked at a railway train map. Or perhaps the map of the London Underground lines. Consider in these contexts how each line connects to another line, sometimes overlapping, sometimes ending. However, each station (belief) is in turn connected to another. No stations are left unconnected, or else no train would be able to travel along the track, and some stations are the main terminus points, at the centre of many lines.

In the same way, every belief within our mind will always need to be connected to another belief. Technical reasons will be given later but, for now, accept that this is true. You will find clear explanations as your reading progresses.

2.3 What is a belief?

In the English Oxford Dictionary you will find that a belief is defined as follows:

belief n.: *1. The mental action, condition, or habit, of trusting to or confiding in a person or thing; trust, dependence, reliance, confidence, faith.*

2. Mental acceptance of a proposition, statement, or fact, as true, on the ground of authority or evidence; assent of the mind to a statement, or to the truth of a fact beyond observation, on the testimony of another, or to the fact or truth on the evidence of consciousness; the mental condition involved in this assent.

3. The thing believed; the proposition or set of propositions held true; opinion, persuasion.

4. A formal statement of doctrines believed, a creed.

5. Confident anticipation, expectation.

Many of the beliefs which you or your clients have will be found to be self-evident. That is, the thoughts which have created the beliefs will have been installed in recent years. However, there will often be cases when, because the originating thoughts were formed many years ago, you may well have forgotten these and consigned them to the lower reaches of your unconscious mind.

However, what happens when the dictionary is out of date, or is a translation from a foreign language and someone has made a mistake? Or if someone, by accident or on purpose, has placed the wrong definitions against the wrong words?

3. How Beliefs Are Formed

3.1 Our childhood years

During our early developmental childhood years we are in a very precarious position. On the one hand we will give total and unconditional love to our key role models (usually our mother and father) and will do whatever we can to keep them happy. Whereas, on the other hand, we haven't as yet learned whether that which they want us to be, say or do is fair or right or appropriate.

This means that we will often unwittingly accept certain ways of thinking or behaving as absolute and correct. This can and does significantly limit our development as we grow up. While in this developmental period, we are collecting and sifting information at a prodigious rate. As children we are fascinated by this new world which we have only recently entered. Every day is new, special and different. Everything we see, feel, hear, smell and taste is accepted absolutely and without any filters of questioning at all.

In addition to this external sensory input, we can also imagine from within certain things. Now it's not important whether you can't or whether you can imagine some of those early memories but you can know that they are still there, somewhere in the inner reaches of your unconscious mind.

3.2 We start making assumptions from an early age

Consider for a moment the scenario of a baby who, quite naturally and automatically, without thinking, cries when he is hungry or wants his nappy changed. Let us assume for a moment that the baby's mother became increasingly angry with the amount of crying that the baby did and felt anger towards the baby because of his crying. While the baby would not consciously understand what the feeling from his mother was, the baby would begin to experience the anger being directed towards him. This feeling of anger would create fear in the baby and the baby, naturally confused by this, would then begin to believe that he should not signal to have his needs met, since this upsets mummy and a little baby knows to do whatever it takes not to upset mummy.

Since this would be a very early and upsetting memory, it would probably be forgotten by the child as he grows up. However, this incident was so powerful that the child would create a belief about not expressing the feelings associated with needing something. This would continue to affect his personality in the present.

3.3 We accept what we are told as true

In the same way, as we grow up and venture out into the world outside the safety of our parents home we continue to accept information in an unquestioning manner. This applies to all information received, whether positive and negative. Consider for a moment how children usually learn, by rote, automatically and without thinking. This is the way that children take in information, automatically, believing naively all that is said to them.

While all of this information is being received, there have been no mechanisms or procedures developed within our minds to answer such questions as, *"Is this right"*, or *"Is this true?"* or, *"Is this fair?"*. As children we have not learnt how to criticise, either constructively or destructively, and therefore we automatically accept EVERYTHING that is suggested to us.

This can be summarised in the phrase below:

"I never get what I want unless what I want is what I am. I am what I think and, therefore, I am my thoughts."

This is a controlled programme that we all have stored within our unconscious minds and this can be, in turn, expressed as follows:

... I am, what I think I am, I am, what I think, I am ...

Consider for a moment the following questions:

Did you as a child believe in Father Christmas?

Did you believe that when you lost a tooth, fairies would place a coin under your pillow while you slept?

Did you ever believe that life would never be the same again for you when your favourite group split up?
Did you ever believe, at least for a while, that if you said you hated your aunt/uncle, that they would never love you again?

Did you ever believe that, because of an argument with him or her, your best friend would never ever play with you again?

It is while we, as children, are in this very sensitive and delicate phase of our development that we all have many things suggested to us. Each one of these messages, suggestions, imagined responses and comments become connected to other previously-accepted memories and are all stored away in the unconscious mind.

It is worthwhile acknowledging once again where the majority of our formative beliefs come from - our parents. They will, in turn, have received their childhood beliefs from their parents. Imagine for a moment what happens to the small child when his father, who was poorly treated by his parents (but has repressed this), treats his son in a similar cold and unfeeling manner. Naturally the child will become discomforted but he will also accept that this is the right way to behave.

3.4 An analogy

It's like Dad giving Son a disk for his computer and telling him that all the information on it is correct, up-to-date and usable. Dad believes it. So Son believes it. But Dad's been carrying that disk of data around for a long time. He's never checked to see whether new programs exist which can operate smoother or better or are perhaps more user-friendly. Perhaps he didn't know about, or didn't even bother to check whether the disk contained a computer virus. Son doesn't know where the disk came from.

(Perhaps it was from a dud batch, perhaps stolen, perhaps damaged.)

We've all heard of computer viruses, those programs which attach themselves covertly to other programs and slowly eat away at the fabric of our computer's memory and capabilities. Well, often people just don't realise that they are installing these inappropriate viruses since they don't have a way of seeing them. Perhaps they've decided to upload a massive chunk of information and hidden in there is a real stinker of a file. But since they trust the person that they've obtained the data from ... well, they would never expect this to happen.

And what is also possible is that the person from whom this important and powerful information was taken didn't realise that what they were offering was corrupt. So they may continue to spread this information, without realising that it is full of hidden flaws. Flaws that would slowly begin to impact on and reduce the quality of life for those in receipt.

3.5 The Law of Belief

Within the unconscious mind there exists an operating system which governs how every one of our thoughts and situations is collated and combined with those already present. This law is known as **The Law of Belief.**

The Law of Belief is a natural law which states that whatever I believe my mind always achieves for me either in reality or with my imagination as fantasy.

In addition, as children we have, naturally, a childlike innocence which means we are capable of amazing levels of imagination and a naive way of believing absolutely what we are told or what we hear or what we perceive. It is only later on as we grow up that we learn to ask questions in order to interpret with clarity the situations around us.

Consider how much more effective your reasoning abilities would have been as a child if you could have asked these types of questions at key times in your life:

Is this right?

Should I feel guilty?

Why do I feel that am I to blame?

Do my parents love me, or do they love what I do?

Do my parents not love me, or is it only that they don't love what I do?

Do they really care about me?

Are they fair?

Are they manipulating me?

Why do they do this to me if they say they love me?

Who are they really trying to protect - me or themselves?

This inability to interpret cleanly means that we will take on messages from other people without thinking that they may be manipulating us or emotionally abusing us. This in turn causes us as children to develop beliefs about how other people will treat us.

This chain-reaction effect can be summarised as:

> **... thoughts give birth to ideas, which give birth
> to new thoughts, which give birth to new ideas ... .**

Once a thought has been thought it can never be unthought. Thought can, however, be reviewed and altered and perceived in a different way.

The effects of this chain-reaction can be seen in clients who have had very domineering parents and who then go on to develop symptoms such as a lack of confidence. During initial questioning it will usually be found that while they do find most people bossy or domineering, they also EXPECT people to be like this. Until this chain of expectation leading to results is broken, they will continue to expect this and, naturally, this is what will happen in many of their interactions.

4. How Beliefs Are Organised Within The Mind

4.1 Overview

As discussed in Chapter 3, thoughts, ideas and images come into our minds from a myriad of sources. Once these have been accepted into our unconscious mind, the mind simplifies each of these records by carrying out a process similar to the process used to create the synopsis for a book.

Think for a moment about what a synopsis is intended to give you. It aims to sum up and condense in an abridged form the overall meaning and message of the book. From the synopsis, provided it has been worded correctly, one should be able to understand the writer's viewpoint and the ideas which he wants to put across.

4.2 The mind always aims to simplify

This is similar to the way in which the mind operates. Each thought is processed and once the synopsis has been created, it is automatically and in an instant connected to other thoughts related to similar subjects. It is from this framework of combined thoughts that beliefs are formed. The reason the mind operates in this way is because it simplifies everything. Rather than have to re-evaluate every situation to understand what it means now, it files every experience it has ever received in a simplified manner, and assumes that it means the same now as it did in the past.

Let us take the example of a girl who was to become so upset and distraught when, after an argument over a toy, her best friend said, *"If you don't let me have what I want, I'll never be your friend again"*. Feeling emotionally confused over what to do, she could have become compelled to give into her friend's threat. As time progressed, she could connect to this belief other similarly-coded instances, each containing a theme such as, *"I must do what others want, even if I don't feel it's right or fair."*

Following the acceptance of the belief by the unconscious mind, the unconscious mind will then use this belief structure to assist it in assimilating further information. This is quite sensible since having already simplified many memories under the same heading of a belief, it can now use the belief to sift and sort additional thoughts and sensory inputs as they arise. However, once the belief is created it in turn becomes a mechanism to be used by the unconscious mind to sort and categorise further thoughts and sensory inputs.

Our teachings from NLP mean we should all be aware that billions of cellular activities are taking place within our bodies every second and that in consequence the unconscious mind will aim to simplify as much as possible through the development of belief structures. (This is defined within NLP as the processes of Distortion, Deletion and Generalisation.) (Bandler & Grinder 1975)

Furthermore, once the framework is in place, the unconscious mind will fight to keep it there, since to change it could well mean a drastic revision of the interpretation it has placed (remember the book synopsis) on many memories. Especially when one considers how long the belief may have been in place and since that time experiences will have occurred which corroborate the belief.

4.3 Sources of influence

A further element in the equation is from whom it was that those original beliefs were generated. This is usually, though not always, parents, teachers, other members of the family or other significant role models. The high regard in which we held these people, or perhaps the revulsion which we felt towards them, will dictate how easy it is to change the beliefs once installed. Sometimes, the people which we held in the highest regard are those which we later find out are those which influenced us the most detrimentally. Other sources of beliefs can be cartoons, magazines, films or even games we play at school.

It is important to acknowledge that during your formative years, every-thing can and may well influence you as a child. Positive incidents will influence you, negative incidents will influence you, and also things that you may feel ambivalent about will influence you. This last category is very important, since, these areas of your experience that you have chosen to become neutral about may contain painful learnings.

As an example, consider how a boy would feel if he were repeatedly let down by his father who keeps 'forgetting' to make the time to watch him play football at school. Of course the reasons would be valid enough to the father - business trips or meetings and so on - and the son may well accept these reasons. However, this son, as he grows up to become a father, could well develop an attitude of mind whereby he is quite casual about his children's sports events, since this allows him to cover over the pain he felt as a young boy.

4.4 Primary Beliefs and Secondary Beliefs

Once a belief structure has been created within the mind, it will seek out and attach itself to other beliefs - those which are most appropriate to the underlying message contained within the original belief. It will seek out within the mind other beliefs with which it will have some affinity or similarity. Once this happens these beliefs will join together, forming a belief complex, which will, in turn, seek out other beliefs to bond with.

This ongoing procedure of beliefs seeking to bond with like beliefs which in turn look for further beliefs, can be analogised with the way in which a cancerous tumour will grow at an exponential rate and can destroy in a short time unless drastic action is taken. Or how an antidote, if administered in time, will destroy the most poisonous chemicals that may have been inadvertently introduced into the body.

This is a natural and eminently practical thing for the unconscious mind to do. This process means the unconscious mind is always simplifying and sorting itself and its surroundings to reduce the number of processes it needs to carry out.

The unconscious mind further simplifies its procedures by sorting beliefs into Primary Beliefs and Secondary Beliefs. Primary Beliefs are the main beliefs, those which actually underpin the whole belief structure. These are usually the memories with the greatest emotional weight and usually, although not always, the oldest.

As an example, let us use the case of a man in his 40s, single and with a weight problem. We have asked him to list for us on a the beliefs he has on weight. (The process to obtain this information is clarified in Section Two).

He writes down the following items:

A Scared of food

B Fear at dinner

C Fat

D Conversation

E Ugly

F Permission

G Grown-ups

H Spots

When asked to connect these beliefs together, the following structure was obtained:

A Scared of food   **B**

B Fear at dinner   **A**

C Fat   A

D Conversation   G

E Ugly   A

F Permission   D

G Grown ups   B

H Spots   D

This can be seen when one presents his thoughts about weight in a pictorial format as a GOLD Counselling™ belief map.

Weight

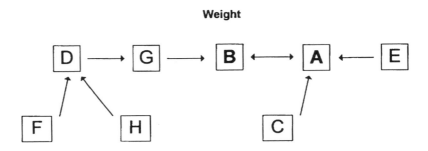

Without having to identify where his beliefs about weight were formed we already know from this that his two Primary Beliefs are **A** and **B**. His Secondary Beliefs (or lower order beliefs) all are in place to support these. Once his Primary Beliefs are revised, the whole of his beliefs about weight will be affected.

5. *The Theory Of Dual Or Multiple States*

5.1 Everything has at least two states of being

Within this chapter we have set out the most important elements which have been brought together to create GOLD Counselling™. We have incorporated herein the specific understandings of which you will be required to develop an awareness if you are to become successful as a GOLD Counsellor™. This element is the concept that we are always switching states, or emotions. One of the iron laws of nature is that everything can be in one of two states. However thinly you divide an object, there are always two sides to it. It can be night or day. A tide flows in or out. Someone may feel happy or sad.

To take a physical example, consider the method by which we use our eyes to see. Even when we focus on one point, our eyes are still moving, left-right, up-down, assessing the situation. These movements, known as saccadic movements are essential to the proper functioning of vision. Without these regular small movements we could not take in visual information.

Another example is breathing. You cannot breath out and in at the same time. The operating system does not permit this. Even pain is not constant. If you were to ask a patient or a doctor to describe pain he will use many different definitions and words to fine-tune the experience, but all will agree that it comes and goes, that it gets stronger then weaker. I am sure that you have been in a condition with a pain that was troubling you but after a while it just seemed to disappear. Later, however, it returned, back to the original strength.

5.2 Emotions change constantly

Within the unconscious mind, in exactly the same way, a thought will never exist on its own; each thought will always be connected to another thought within the belief structure. The rationale behind the way in which the unconscious mind sorts information is very important. Every belief structure will contain two or more beliefs, all of which are structured according to their level of *emotional* content.

In order to clarify this important point further, let us now consider the example of someone who was asked to list all the different things he feels that he does. Let us assume that a list of activities was generated as follows:

Work, Play, Eat, Drink, Fight, Make love, Sulk, Visit parents, Drive, Teach children, Cook, Travel, Sleep, Wash.

From reviewing this list, we can assume certain things. One thing is that it is unlikely that someone would be carrying out all of these activities at the same time. Therefore, he will need to swap roles or states as required. Perhaps he could be working and, at the same time, eating, drinking or travelling. However, he could not work while visiting parents. Neither could he carry out any of the former states while sleeping.

If we now take this idea a step further, let us generate a list of possible emotional states that one could enter. One possible list could appear as follows;

Happy, Sad, Aroused, Dejected, Sleepy, Bored, Jolly, Angry, Passionate, Melancholic, Delighted, Sentimental, Thrilled, Upset, Elated, and Lonely.

Most people will have experienced some or all of these states in the past. When we review the list we can see that the different states can be divided into two distinct groups as follows:

Happy	Sad
Aroused	Dejected
Sleepy	Bored
Jolly	Angry
Passionate	Melancholic
Delighted	Sentimental
Thrilled	Upset
Elated	Lonely

While we acknowledge that the above division of emotions is arbitrary, we would suggest that there are clearly certain emotions which are positive and others which are negative.

If we elaborate further, one would not be able to experience any of these emotions within the second list while experiencing any of those in the first. It's as if one's mind is incapable of feeling *angry* while feeling *elated*. Or *delighted* while being *lonely*.

5.3 Emotional change always follows a sequence

Within our unconscious minds we all have a type of syntax which controls what feelings we experience and when. This means that we may switch in an instant from one state to another. Perhaps you can remember a time when one minute you felt great and the next something seemed to happen inside you and the feeling changed to one of frustration, or sadness, or whatever else you may have felt?

If you were able to stop and analyse the circular sequence that your emotions flow through, you would be able to recognise that they always follow the same broad pattern. Perhaps you might feel elated, then self-conscious, then feel guilty for feeling so good, then seem to get stuck with guilt for quite a while.

Let us take an example which permits us to consider in more detail how we cross these emotional thresholds. Do you know of someone, or are you perhaps someone whom people say the following about. *"That guy, he just seems so cold at times, it's as if he doesn't realise how hurtful what he says is to me. He doesn't seem to do it on purpose, he just doesn't seem to notice what he's doing."*

In this scenario, this man has unconsciously created specific mechanisms within his mind which facilitate the following:

1. A belief structure about how to act with other people, in respect of treating them with empathy, based on previously real or imagined experiences within his own life.

2. A filtering mechanism which does not flag up any emotional responses from other people which are below a certain level.

This filtering mechanism can be seen when we consider how he would respond if challenged over his attitude. Probably he would not even realise that he was being cold, callous or suchlike, since these states are themselves beliefs about what those feelings are.

He may initially feel anger at having his approach challenged in this manner. Other people may attempt to play "the blame game" focusing attention on others and away from themselves.

5.4 How the sequence is created

Whenever a new belief is received it is incorporated into the existing structure by a process known as *Matching*. Take, for example, a child who is praised and feels proud. That feeling of *proud* may become matched to its nearest counterpart, for example, that of feeling **confident**. However, the actual structure will be determined by the level of emotional content which is contained within the memories.

This means that the belief structure will be organised around a framework of *Primary Beliefs* and *Secondary Beliefs*. The unconscious mind will achieve this since it will then be able to focus its energy on fulfilling the Primary Beliefs which, in turn, continue to ensure that the Secondary Beliefs (or lower order beliefs) are fulfilled.

6. How The Unconscious Mind Controls Our Behaviour

6.1 How we learn

Scientific discoveries have now enabled us to develop an understanding of the way in which many and varied automatic functions are carried out within our bodies. We now know that it is the unconscious mind which controls most of our automatic functions. This includes the deep, genetically-programmed drives, such as those for survival and procreation, and the simpler, learned, habitual patterns which are taught from an early age.

Most authorities acknowledge that our learning process can be defined as comprising four distinct steps. Each of which uses the conscious and unconscious mind in different ways. Furthermore, if we recognise that we are all learning new ways of behaving and adding these to those which we already know, then it follows that we can be at one or more of these different stages at the same time, depending on what we are doing at that time.

1. *UNCONSCIOUS INCOMPETENCE*: This occurs when we don't know what we don't know. We can be anything from a child not knowing he doesn't know how to walk, because he has not tried it yet, to a person who has not realised that there is a better way of planning the day.

2. *CONSCIOUS INCOMPETENCE*: During this stage we now know what we don't know. Consider the same child's frustration now when he tries and fails to co-ordinate his limbs in order to stand on two legs and walk. Or that same person who can recognise that other people in the office are achieving more in less time and with less stress.

3. *CONSCIOUS COMPETENCE*: We have now identified and are learning the steps and processes to carry out the tasks that previously we found impossible. These tasks could range from walking or making toast through to driving a car or piloting an aircraft. During this learning phase, we have to filter everything through our conscious mind which means that we will process information at a slower pace than we would like. This could also include driving to a new place of work. This is a phase of frustration as we learn the right way from the

wrong way. This will show up in the expression of concentration on the child's face as he attempts to consciously manipulate his muscles and to co-ordinate his body movements. The elation from success would also be noticed at this stage.

4. *UNCONSCIOUS COMPETENCE:* Once we have been able to master the specific processes, we can now consign the physical and emotional tasks to the unconscious mind. From this stage on, we will not notice ourselves carrying out the steps. Someone would state that he does what he does automatically and without thinking. This includes such examples as the young child who is now able to walk with fluidity and is quite nonchalant about the process. Or finding that taking the formerly-new journey to the office has become an automatic process and that we no longer notice certain signs or road junctions as we used to.

Once a learning has passed into the final stage we will no longer notice what is being thought or carried out, nor will we ever consciously stop to question how or why we are thinking as we are.

Clearly, the more quickly and easily a task, or a way of behaving, or a way of thinking, can be taken up to Level 4, *Unconscious Competence*, the more simplified someone will find his life. Provided, of course, that the methodology which he consigns to the deeper recesses of his unconscious mind is useful to him and has not been based on limiting incorrect beliefs.

It is the belief structures about how to act, think and do things which become consigned to our unconscious mind, which we, as therapists, deal with on a day-to-day basis. Naturally, we can, if necessary, create significant improvements in a client's learning process but we will usually find it necessary to assist the client in revising his beliefs about his attitudes first.

6.2 How the unconscious mind filters out information

The conscious mind is that part of our mind which is used to process the thinking of which we are aware. This includes such things as reading the words of this book, taking notice of the sounds outside the room, or actually carrying on a conversation. This part of our mind cannot do many things at once and various tests have indicated that the maximum number of discrete activities which can be administered by the conscious mind is seven, plus or minus two, depending on complexity.

The unconscious mind, however, has an amazingly large capacity to operate in a multi-tasking way since every other function within the human body is carried out, timed and monitored by the unconscious mind. This part of our mind can and does complete millions and millions of tasks per second. And of these, there are probably very few of which we are ever aware.

While sitting and reading this book, turning pages as you go, have you *consciously* caused or *consciously* noticed any of these things happening?

the turning of the page

adjustments in your seating position

blinking

understanding what each word in the text of the book meant to you

the instantaneous connection of some of these meanings to your own experiences

the ongoing process of ensuring that your breathing continues, that your heart beats and so on

All of these activities and functions will have been carried out by the direct or indirect action of different parts of your unconscious mind. In exactly the same way, your unconscious mind will have filtered all of your thoughts, memories and experiences so as to save you the trouble of having to go "back to basics" each time. Consider how much more difficult it would be for you if every time you were to read a word you had to look up its definition in a dictionary. No. Once you know what a word means, you accept its meaning as correct each time. This is similar to the way in which beliefs operate.

7. The Relationship Between Energy And Thought

7.1 A quantum viewpoint

Modern scientific research indicates that at the lowest level of form, that of the quantum, we don't exist. If we use this book as an example we can appreciate the mind-boggling effects of this statement. This book contains pages, pages are made of paper, paper contains molecules, molecules are comprised of atoms, atoms are bundles of energy when you approach the quantum level, and energy is 99.9999% absolute nothing, empty space.

It therefore follows that everything is made up of energy and also everything nearly totally doesn't exist.

Science has also provided us with further information on energy. Energy cannot be created or destroyed. It can only be changed, channelled or converted - in this context, through aligning and focusing a person's beliefs from multiple directions to a single direction. From this he will be able to achieve his desires from a position of ease, rather than fail from a position of tiredness and stress.

7.2 Mental energy

Most people are aware of how it is to feel physically exhausted but many do not believe that you can really be mentally exhausted. But by under-standing how a belief structure operates and that the unconscious mind is burning up energy all the time to fulfil each and every belief, it is possible to become aware of how mental exhaustion occurs.

Energy is expended all the time, whether we are awake or asleep. A tremendous amount of energy can be expended when we are asleep, especially after significant changework has occurred, which then requires integration within the unconscious mind.

However, once we have assisted the client in realigning his beliefs so that all his beliefs for a single issue are congruent and focused in the same direction, he will find that he will use less energy to complete his tasks. Naturally, this energy now available may become used elsewhere and he

is now presented with choice. He is no longer *"running around like a headless chicken"* (which was how one client expressed his previous lifestyle).

This change in the client's belief structure ensures that the appropriate behavioural change results and, in doing so, alleviates the client's confu-sion. This will usually show up the underlying beliefs which have been operating out of the client's conscious awareness and causing the problems in his life.

7.3 How a belief draws energy towards itself

Once a belief has been set in place, it will start to grow. The more emotionally powerful the originating incident was, the more energy the belief will have to start with. However, any and all beliefs will grow over time, be they positive or negative. This occurs through the client's unconscious processes which will draw into his life those events which each belief needs to stay continually fulfilled. As this happens, more and more energy becomes contained within the belief structure, as more and more thoughts become consolidated as one single structure.

If we consider for a moment the structure of a belief system, we find that it looks surprisingly similar to the format used to explain how atoms join together. The similarity is continued further when we recognise a further fact - the thoughts and beliefs closer to the centre have more emotional energy than those at the outer reaches. The significance of this fact is that your client is using an ever-increasing amount of energy all the time that he is fulfilling his beliefs.

This is similar to the property of mutual attraction possessed by all bodies that are made of matter. Science has revealed that the more dense an object is, the larger the gravitational force created - in turn drawing objects towards itself. Similarly, within a belief structure, two or more highly emotionally-charged Primary Beliefs at the centre of the structure will cause other thoughts and experiences to become attracted to them and these will in turn create Secondary Beliefs (or lower order beliefs).

This is self-perpetuating since the belief structure will be stronger and more able to draw towards itself thoughts and experiences from other structures, further increasing its own energy levels. This process can be analogised to the way in which a black hole, which is an extremely dense body, draws every type of energy towards itself, consuming more and more matter as it becomes heavier and heavier.

To explain how this would operate in a real situation, let us consider the example of someone who has a belief, formed in childhood, that he needs to be rejected. Until he identifies the originating cause and releases the pent up emotional energy, he will, unconsciously, always seek rejection. This will take a lot of time and energy to do. If, however, he were to find a partner who has a belief about never standing up for her rights, we have now an accident waiting to happen. The first person will be expending energy attempting to create situations whereby his partner will reject him, and his partner will be burning up energy in an attempt to keep them together. As time moves on these two people will generate more and more friction between them, both attempting to fulfil their ill-matched beliefs. Sooner or later something must give. This could be in the form of a thera-peutic change, separation, illness or violence. One thing we can be sure of - the unreleased emotional energy will find a way out.

7.4 Lying is tiring

When we say the right thing to please others, even when we know it's not true, we suppress the release of emotional energy. Until released this will continue to stay within our body and will effect our day-to-day life in various ways.

When you are in a position whereby you must choose between what is and what should be, the mind will always choose to focus on what should be. This difference between reality and imagination will require further energy to keep the lie going, further draining your client's energy levels and possibly creating psychosomatic illnesses.

However, once your client is able to have an emotional release of the belief which is the lie, he will never need to hold on to that lie again. From then on, his energy levels will begin to rebuild and, as stated in Section 7.2, his new alignment will ensure he draws positive and not negative experiences into his life.

7.5 The self-organising system within the unconscious mind

It is, from this stage onwards, appropriate to consider and recognise that the unconscious mind processes beliefs as if they are each living structures, equivalent to a totally self-organising system. The unconscious mind controls and organises the overall structure and prioritises beliefs according to the type and strength of emotional content. This is because every thought, sensory input or memory once had a level of emotional input which is the prime element used by the unconscious mind to sort thoughts into beliefs.

Our research has meant that we have been able to design a process diagram which sets out exactly how the unconscious mind operates when it creates a belief structure. The flowchart overleaf sets out the methodology which is used by the unconscious mind when doing this.

The unconscious mind is receiving new thoughts, ideas and sensory inputs all the time. Every one of these is either added to an existing belief structure, or is used with at least one other thought to create a new belief structure.

It can be seen that the unconscious mind applies a very simple but powerful sort program every time a new thought occurs. This means that it can efficiently and effectively sort and collate hundreds of thousands of thoughts. Under normal circumstances, we are only ever aware of a few thoughts - those with an emotional content above a certain level.

Flowchart to explain how a belief structure is created from individual thoughts

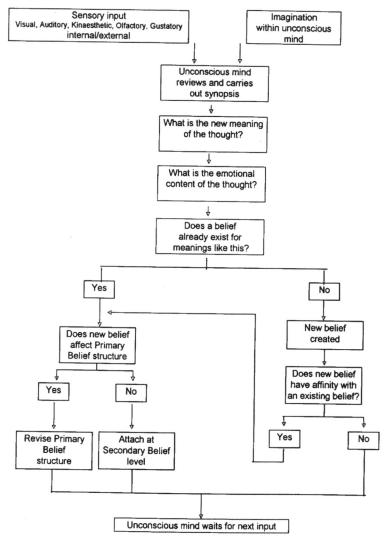

Flowchart to explain how a belief structure is created from individual thoughts

8. How Thoughts Are Remembered

8.1 What is a true memory?

How do you know that you know that you're right in what you remember? How do you know that you know that your memory hasn't failed you? When *The Independent* newspaper was launched in the mid 1980s, a series of television adverts showed just how easy it is for a group of people all watching the same incident to have different memories about it. Consider the scene. A frail old man is walking along the pavement. Suddenly, a dangerous-looking youth, shaven-headed and in jeans runs towards him and, just as the old man reaches the corner, the youth pushes him out of the way.

Next we cut to a different angle. In this we see a uniformed police officer running towards the youth. It seems that he is giving chase. And lastly, we are then presented with a wider-angled perspective. We see that both the youth and the policeman are both running towards the same old man. This is because the scaffolding above him has given way and in seconds he would be crushed beneath steel and rubble. Both were risking their lives to save his.

"The Independent. It is, are you?" was the by-line. Only when you've been able to assimilate all the facts is it possible to determine the truth, but by whose definition is it the truth?

Facts are facts but interpretations are different. Consider how the legal system works. Both sides will aim to present cases which show their clients in the best light. Both are "true" and a jury is required to determine which truth is to be believed.

Where this is important for a therapist is that the memories which a client has are just that - memories. No-one can prove these memories are right or wrong. They are purely an interpretation of events. Our role is to ensure that the events can be interpreted, or sometimes reinterpreted, by our clients so as to release any limitations which the original view may have caused.

8.2 Emotional content

Most people are more able to remember things in which they have had an emotional involvement. It's as if emotions are the filter which is applied to determine whether the memory is stored with a lot of detail or with minimal detail. Consider two different meals in a restaurant. One you have with friends you value greatly, one is with someone you find, frankly, quite boring. With the first event you will no doubt be able to recollect in greater detail and more easily the various facets of the event. Whereas in the second, its lack of emotional content renders the incident forgettable.

Another reason for thoughts or incidents to become stored is when the event was felt to be so important, so monumental to you that it actually altered your beliefs about the world. Consider how comfortable someone may feel walking along the same road on the way home from work for years, until on one particular day he is robbed at knife-point. This incident would be personal, emotionally very powerful, new and different and force him to reconsider his beliefs in respect of personal safety. As a result this information would definitely become stored as a long-term memory, whether or not he can consciously remember the incident. Recognise that whether you consciously attempt to repress and deny the memory will not matter at all. Once the memory has been laid down within your mind it will influence you thereafter.

8.3 The affects of ageing

Most scientists involved in the research as to the way in which the human brain operates believe that we appear to utilise a small amount of the total volume available. Also, it is believed that if taught correctly, we can learn a phenomenal amount at an amazing rate. So why then is it that as people grow older, their capability to learn diminishes. It's certainly not because they've run out of space in their heads! Consider how some professors continue in their teaching posts for years, often long after their retirement, and their subjects are invariably cerebral, not physical.

The reason is due to the beliefs which have already been formed within that person at an earlier time. To use an analogy to explain, let us consider the petrol gauge in a car. This operates by picking up information in the petrol tank as to the level of capacity in the tank. Too much and one could run out of fuel. Too little capacity and you've got a full tank. But what would happen if the wrong sender was fitted. Say a sender for an 8-gallon

tank on a 10-gallon car? The gauge on the dashboard would always understate the capacity left over. Obviously when filling up at a petrol station this error may be noticed but, all the time one is reading the instruments in the car, the error would be compounded.

And this is what happens with people as they age. It is usual to learn at school. Afterwards, most people will seek employment and then spend the majority of their years working not learning. Because this is the accepted way of thinking and behaving, this is what happens. If you were to review the beliefs of older, retired people about learning, you would identify significant limiters as to being too old, not my place, letting the youngsters have a go, and so on. In doing so they are fulfilling their beliefs, which are that as they've become older they could not learn anymore. Many times older people use the phrase "You can't teach an old dog new tricks" as an attempt to justify the reason why they don't want to change. As therapists we must recognise this for what it really is. They are saying "can't" when they really mean "won't". This is a belief and this would need to be questioned and revised before change will occur.

A further example of how age and beliefs are inter-related can be revealed when considering the effects of retirement on the male population. Some men look forward to retirement since to them it means that they can do new things with their new-found time. Whereas others not long after retirement find themselves succumbing to illness, boredom and listlessness. It's as if, to them, to retire from work is to retire from life.

8.4 Every thought influences

Every single event which we have experienced, either by our external senses, such as sight or touch, or our internal senses, including anything we have imagined or dreamt, will have influenced us in some way. Some events may have become less important as we have grown up or changed our social situations but at different times in our lives every thought must have at some time influenced us.

To elaborate further on this, consider not only how effective but also how subtle some advertising is. Most adverts don't sell purely the object for which you will be handing over your hard-earned money. No. They sell you the image, how you imagine you will look/feel/behave/be treated by others because you have wisely chosen their product. In a single day of travelling through an average town we are bombarded by hundreds, if not thousands, of different adverts. Each one will generate thoughts in our mind, either positive, negative or neutral. All of these thoughts come together to form a picture of what you like or dislike and so on and once you have purchased the product - you in turn become an advert. This means that the personality which you develop may be influenced in ways by sources which you didn't even realise were there.

8.5 Memory is not accurate

Lying takes so much time and takes up so much energy. Most people just don't remember everything and when you read about the mental feats of people who memorise lists of numbers you can realise that specific techniques are required. It, therefore, follows that most people will not record everything with clarity. Often we quite honestly can't remember something. So we have to skirt around it, remembering bits at a time, until the whole memory is reformed once again. However, if a story were fabricated all that would exist in someone's mind would be the framework he had built.

Often, when remembering a memory we notice that something about the same memory is now different. This flexibility in recall is a natural phenomenon and through applying relaxation techniques to remove further blockages to recall, even more detail can be ascertained.

8.6 Types of memory

Research shows that we all appear to have different types of memory and that one or more types are used whenever we consign an event to our unconscious mind. Understanding which type is being presented by your client will ensure that you can achieve clarity when he is, consciously or not, putting up barriers to recall.

1. **EVENT MEMORY** is the ability to recall an incident at a particular time, in a particular place.

2. **ROTE MEMORY** occurs when something has been carried out so many times that differences between each occasion have been lost. This is more vague than event memory and can apply when one of the events was distressing.

3. **PERIOD MEMORY** occurs when someone only seems to have a feeling about a large amount of time, perhaps feeling that all school was boring or lonely. This has obviously a large number of individual memories bundled together and can be influenced by a desire not to delve too deeply into the past.
4. **SCENIC MEMORY** occurs when someone has a memory of a place, such as a house he has lived in, but only experiences it visually. To expand this we would need to encourage him to access information from his mind about what he might be seeing, hearing or feeling.

5. **SCREEN MEMORY** happens when we think we know why we feel or act the way we do, whereas this is really a displacement, a substitution for the real reason. This may occur due to the negative effects of positive thinking, (see Chapter 11) or due to ongoing symptom-substitution, or denial.

6. **FUZZY MEMORY** effects occur when the unconscious mind fills in missing parts of information with that which it believes to be true, even though there is no justification for its actions.

It is not always realised how powerful the unconscious mind's desire to simplify its actions really is. This is embodied within the concept of Fuzzy Memory. You can carry out a simple experiment to experience first-hand how Fuzzy Memory effects all of us.

Take a piece of white A4 paper and mark on it two black circles. Now choose either one and make a hole through it. Next, hold the paper by either of the bottom corners and close one eye. Slowly bring the sheet of paper towards your face while focusing your other open eye on the black spot. Keep aware of the hole using peripheral vision and notice what happens as you bring the sheet closer. At a certain distance the hole will "disappear". In fact, your unconscious mind has assumed that this area is as solid, as is the rest of the paper, and fills in the missing information for you. However, it is wrong. This is what the unconscious mind will do with memories causing you to believe certain things when, in fact, they are fabrications from your own unconscious mind.

8.7 Tricks of the eye - the desire for simplicity

Once we believe something to be true, we will unconsciously look for ways to prove it so. Furthermore, we will often see and experience things, not as they are but as we expect them to be. Many automatic patterns are built up in this way.

We are sure that most of you reading this book will have seen examples of those pictures which are designed to trick the eye. One minute the image is of a candlestick and, the next, you can see two faces looking at each other. Or perhaps you have seen some of the graphics created by the artist M. C. Esher. He used the two dimensions of paper to distort the reader's viewpoint and create apparently impossible situations such as water running uphill, never-ending staircases, or rooms without separate inside walls or outside walls.

Many people use this technique outside their driveways when they put up a notice, in blue which says "POLITE NOTICE - NO PARKING". The mind expects to see POLICE and, therefore, that is what we believe we see.

9. *Language, Words And Speech*

9.1 The need for communication

It is fascinating to consider that every civilisation which has ever inhabited our planet at whatever time in its history has felt the need to develop ways of recording the things which it has felt, heard or seen. From such diverse places as cave paintings, stone tablets, papyrus roles and village chants, we have always sought a medium to express how those things that we have experienced have affected us.

Some of these mediums of expression have been focused on the supposed true facts, such as written texts, historical paintings and photographs. Other methods have been developed to enable feelings or abstract interpretations of the writers or artists or designers to be expressed with the hope that they would be understood by others in the same way.

It is this attempt to enable others to understand the meaning within the communication which has been a challenge ever since the earliest days of developing methods of communication. While there has not, as yet, been developed a means of knowing exactly what someone else is feeling, seeing or hearing, by using language in an artful way it is possible to determine what the experience has meant to him.

It therefore follows that dependent on both the level of competence held by the user and the skills available to him, it is possible to clarify the meaning of the experience to a greater or lesser degree.

9.2 Misunderstandings and misinterpretations

Have you ever been in, or can you imagine, a situation whereby in talking to someone you have to correct his interpretation of your words? *"No. That's not what I mean. What I meant was ..."* Or perhaps you have thought you understood someone completely and then realised that his interpretation of events had been distinctly different to yours. Everyone that you ever come into contact with will have had different experiences and will have grown up in different ways. Accordingly, there will be a difference between what you say and how it is understood. Furthermore, words have different meanings to all of us. We use words in an attempt to say what we mean. We will always use our best endeavours to select words which best express the message we want to get across.

Perhaps as children or even as adults you have played games that are designed to connect your skills of word association. This includes such things as "Chinese Whispers" and games in which, by changing contexts, different meanings for words have to be found.

This is one of the reasons why learning a language can become so difficult for some people, because when interacting with others there exists many possibilities for misinterpretations and subsequent justifications.

9.3 The difference between language and words

Within the unconscious mind, a word does not just have a meaning, it has a connection to other words in a linguistic daisy-chain - just as one memory will lead to another and another and so on. If we are able to follow these chains, we are then able to understand the deeper significance which has been attached by the client's unconscious mind to the words which he is using.

This example from an actual session will explain further. A client, who had repressed his emotions, recollects reading Star Trek annuals as a child and imagining himself as Mr Spock. After releasing this memory he later found himself connecting two further incidents which were related to the first by language.

As a teenager, his favourite aircraft was the *Avro Vulcan* and his favourite television series was *The Prisoner*. The client originally believed that he "just liked" the *Vulcan*. Although he made many aircraft models he never once felt the need to build a model of the *Vulcan*. This was his unconscious mind's way of using words to indicate the underlying symptom. In the series *The Prisoner*, the main character was captured and held against his will. The character was very cold and logical, similar to Mr Spock, and for years the client had been interested in purchasing a *Lotus Super 7* - the car used by the character. On further reflection, he realised that he had heard that the character in *The Prisoner* had used the *Lotus* before the client had even seen the series. It was only years later that he actually sat down and watched the series.

Once the underlying cause had been released, along with his need for certain words to be in his mind, his interest in the aircraft and the television series shifted to one of neutrality. This indicated that his attraction to these things was the product of the original way of thinking about feelings and not from other more naturally-explained causes.
This example also reveals that the chronological affect of thoughts within the mind should be measured by reference to the client and not to any external and arbitrary clocks.

This leads us to the pre-supposition that a specific word is that specific word because it is not another - it is different from any other word. A word will have a value because of its difference to others. Furthermore, once something becomes labelled within our minds, we always refer to that label when we are really referring to the object.

9.4 The problem with confusing language and speech

It is important to recognise that there exists significant differences between language and speech and that these differences are of supreme importance when treating clients.

Language is a set of non-verbal symbols used to represent thoughts and feelings. Speech is vocal communication. Another interpretation is that speech is what we use to communicate to others, language is what we use ourselves. There needs to be two or more people for there to be any speech, whereas we can understand language internally.

As soon as someone starts speaking he is unconsciously giving an identity to the person to whom he is talking. Consider also what happens in an alternative scenario whereby someone's identity is taken away from him. A girl is "sent to Coventry" by her classmates because of something she believes she has done wrong. This act of not talking to her removes her from the inter-action of the class and ignores her existence.

As soon as you speak you are, at an unconscious level, selecting from all your thoughts and interpretations of language AND also unconsciously considering the other person as to what to say to him. When a client speaks, therefore, the words he uses have a significance in excess of that which is at first apparent.

This can be captured in the following phrase :

The words I use mean more than I mean in using them.

All speech carries meanings which are below the conscious awareness of the person speaking. Within therapeutic situations, this means that by being able to identify the links in the client's language, and making the appropriate connections, we can facilitate change.

9.5 The link between symptoms and language

Within the unconscious mind, language is used to store our thoughts. In this way, symptoms will be found to relate and link to specific words used by the client.

Although we know that at birth a baby cannot understand language, we know that he can hear language. Consider for a moment if you were on a train and heard two people conversing in a foreign language. While you may not be able to understand what is being said you could hear what is being said. In effect, the language that the baby will come to use exists before the baby does. As a child grows up and can understand language, he will learn to do the things which the words mean.

If we use another example from the work carried out with another client you should then be able to understand how this would come to light in practice. A client had been troubled by problems with money for many years. From the work carried out he seemed always to be waiting and hoping that his family would help him out when he got into financial difficulties. A particular phrase he often used (but didn't notice the significance of himself) was of being "bailed out".

Once he had finally reached financial rock-bottom, he did in fact ask his family for help. The result was exactly what he had hoped would not happen. They refused. They would not help him. Realising this was, for him, initially, a very painful and traumatic experience. However, he was then able to understand that for years he had been waiting, to use his own words "for my ship to come in." As a postscript, he later advised us that while watching television one day when visiting his family, he saw a programme which, in turn, jogged his memory to a series which he used to watch as a child. Its name was *When The Boat Comes In* and was, in his own words, "set in a poor fishing village where no-one had anything of financial value".

Needless to say, the usage of the phrase "bail me out" has stopped.

If we take the concept of symptoms being inextricably linked to words, we can realise their obvious effects in such things as hypochondria. In this, a patient will be convinced that a specific part of his body has a particular problem, even though all medical interventions have denied this fact. By determining the underlying meaning of the words the client is using to denote the area of his body with the problem, the link to the underlying unconscious symptom will be revealed. Once this is brought to the surface of consciousness the symptom will disappear since it is no longer needed.

In this way, the therapist needs to listen for and notice the correlation between the presenting symptoms and the actions which the client takes. The client's unconscious mind will indicate the actual cause of the problem through language and, therefore, we could equate the symptoms with words trapped in his body trying to get out by any means possible.

Section Two:

What is GOLD Counselling™?

Introduction to Section Two

Having read Section One you should now understand how the mind works at a technical level. Within Section Two you will find documented the procedures to use through which it is possible to create a radical shift in a person's beliefs and enable him to instantly and permanently change his beliefs into something empowering instead of restricting.

10. Specific Pre-Supposistions Within GOLD Counselling™

10.1 Overview

Just as with NLP, Transactional Analysis, Gestalt Therapy and Inner-Child Counselling and many other therapeutic approaches, within the framework of the GOLD Counselling™ techniques there are specific pre-suppositions which need to be understood in order to ensure your success with its application.

When you first review these pre-suppositions, some of you may feel that they can't be right, that they seem illogical, impossible even. Well, we have found them *all* to be correct. As you continue to develop your understanding of this method, your realisation will expand to appreciate that each pre-supposition fits exquisitely within each instance of the GOLD Counselling™ techniques applied. We have found these pre-suppositions to be accurate every time and they form the foundations, the building blocks from which the specific techniques have been developed.

By keeping these pre-suppositions close to your awareness while working with your clients, you will understand with much more clarity why it is that certain things may be happening in their lives right now.

The pre-suppositions have been found to divide into two groups: Structural and Functional.

10.2 Structural pre-suppositions

Structural pre-suppositions can be used to identify the way in which the mind combines and collates individual thoughts which are then turned into actual living beliefs. Once these pre-suppositions are understood, you will realise how the unconscious mind will keep together all the various beliefs and ensure that all are fulfilled, at whatever cost.

1. The map *is* the territory. The way in which a person experiences the world is absolutely correct, based on all his experiences from whatever sources. In factual terms it may not be accurate, but it is the way in which he experiences the world and, therefore, that *is* how it is for him.
2. Opposing beliefs *do not* imply a contradiction. The unconscious mind will in one instant fulfil positive, life-enhancing beliefs and then, in a second, change and begin to fulfil negative, even harmful, beliefs without question.

3. There is no pre-set structure or pre-set framework that beliefs form. The brain is a self-organising system and, accordingly, there is no structure - the structure is the structure.

4. The mind is minimalist. It will fulfil *any and all* beliefs using the simplest and most direct way possible.

5. To achieve a goal or feeling or objective, one must first remove the beliefs that are being fulfilled which are exactly 180° in the opposite direction. Rather than add positive thinking, *remove* negative thinking.

6. Every belief cell will contain two or more beliefs, all of which are structured according to its level of *emotional* content.

10.3 Functional pre-suppositions

An understanding of functional pre-suppositions means that the therapist will be able to realise how the mind will continue to fulfil past, present and future beliefs, good, bad or indifferent, until acted on by the GOLD Counselling™ technique.

1. The unconscious mind does not understand past tense. Any beliefs installed in the past are still believed in the present. It only understands what *"is"*, never what *"was"*.

2. The unconscious mind cannot carry out instructions to achieve a state of being in the future tense. Any states or outcomes desired in the future must have already been achieved in the present. It understands only *"is"*, never *"to be"*.

3. The unconscious mind does not think, it just *does*. Automatically and repeatedly until told to do otherwise.

4. We never get what we want unless what we want is what we are. We are what we think and, therefore, we are our thoughts.

5. We live our lives by every belief we have. We are now the sum total of all that we have ever believed.

6. The unconscious mind will fulfil all beliefs within the unconscious mind at all times.

7. *All* thought is creative.

8. In the unconscious mind it is not the event, but rather the *interpretation* of the event, which is stored.

11. Problems With Instilling Positive Thinking

As you now reflect on the pre-suppositions as listed in Chapter 9, it is possible to understand why various other methods, which you may have used to help either yourself or your clients, will have been doomed to failure as time progressed. Perhaps this will also clarify why certain apparent "successes" have turned into "failures" over time.

This would be because no attempt was made to remove the harmful, limiting beliefs which were actually causing the problem. All that occurred was that good, positive beliefs were placed over these. When you understand this, it is possible to realise the folly of so many so-called self-improvement techniques.

However, if it were possible to totally and permanently remove the limiting belief, all that would remain within the person's unconscious mind would be the positive belief, and this would move the person forward to the person which he wishes to become.

But, unfortunately, most of us are unable to identify what it is that is actually limiting us. This is often because the area of our life in which we must look may contain some unpleasant memories; so we elect to cover these up with a dose of positive thinking and get on with trying to do the best we can. To separate these so-called techniques from GOLD Counselling™ we have named these approaches *"Fools Gold"*.

To understand further the problems associated with this approach, imagine what would happen in the following situation. A man buys an old house to live in and to slowly renovate. Initially filled with enthusiasm, he sets himself a schedule to rebuild all the rooms and to carry out whatever is needed to rectify any problems. However, as time moves on, he keeps on finding himself making excuses not to start work in two of the rooms. *"They're not too bad"*, he says. *"Perhaps I'll wait a bit longer"* he thinks. He seems to ignore the fact that these two rooms are both in need of major structural work, and that these are the rooms which contain the strengthening supports for the whole house.

If someone uses these techniques, his approach is like having first bought an old property and then to paper over the cracks in the walls so that they can't be seen. Or instead of removing the roots of weeds in the garden, cutting them down to the surface so that they don't show followed by planting new shrubs in the same ground and hoping that all will be well.

Many of the people with whom we have worked using this technique had already tried many other positive-thinking-based techniques, albeit unsuccessfully. Once they understood how GOLD Counselling™ works they then either dropped the old techniques totally, or incorporated their new learning's into their existing methodologies.

The types of techniques which have within them all the limitations previously mentioned would include such approaches as:

positive thinking
affirmations
progressive de-sensitisation
goal-setting
writing out positive versions of negative beliefs
visualisation
reading motivational literature
suggestion therapy
wishing or hoping
New Year's resolutions
denial, or pretending that those things did not really happen

While all of these approaches can generate partial and short-term successes, no attempt is made to remove the negative belief which is underpinning the existing negative belief structure. Taking the analogy of the old house, eventually the cracks will get worse, connecting to cracks in other parts of the walls. Left unattended, the house itself could become worse and worse, perhaps weakening those nearby.

Exponents of these techniques believe and act as if by taking ten or twenty positive beliefs and using them to smother a few negative beliefs, all will be well.

This approach fails, and it fails because, in itself, it fails to incorporate the learnings embodied in GOLD Counselling™ pre-supposition 10.2.2. Opposing beliefs *do not* imply a contradiction. The unconscious mind will in one instant fulfil positive, life-enhancing beliefs and then, in a second, change and begin to fulfil negative, even harmful, beliefs without question.

Furthermore, in just the same way as when growing a seed from a plant, the seed requires regular tending and nurturing, so do new beliefs. Those already in existence have more power over the newcomers and will further reinforce their influence, sucking energy away from the new ways of thinking.

If, however, someone does appear to derive a benefit from any of the foregoing techniques, then he will have unknowingly caused the symptom to substitute itself into another facet of his life. Take, for example, someone who has a lack of confidence. If he were to recite affirmations which are constructed to tell himself that he is now a confident person, he may well become confident. But over the coming days he may begin to notice a fresh problem rearing its head. Until the originating cause is removed, symptom substitution will continue.

A further danger in using any of these techniques is that by the time a client presents himself for treatment, the symptom that he may consider to be the problem may be as a result of many shifts and displacements from the originating cause. In this way, positive thinking actually worsens the situation, rather than improves it.

This was eloquently expressed by Carl Gustav Jung (1969) who wrote:

> *"A neurosis is truly removed only when it has removed the false attitude of the ego. We do not cure it, it cures us. A man is ill, but the illness is nature's attempt to heal him, and what the neurotic throws away as absolutely worthless contains the **true gold** we should never have found elsewhere."*

12. *The GOLD Counselling™ Language Patterns*

12.1 Overview

As explained within Chapter 9, the language used by a client when explaining his problem will provide us with an enormous amount of information about his symptoms and the underlying causes. Therefore by understanding what the language used by your client actually means, not only to him as he understands it but also at a deeper unconscious level, we can identify where change needs to occur.

12.2 Language patterns

If you have an appreciation of the importance that language holds within NLP, you will no doubt expect that within GOLD Counselling™ a specific language pattern has been developed to ensure the success of the technique. The precise language which is used is important since inappropriate guidance by the therapist would effect the direction along which the analysis progresses.

For example, if a particular belief such as *"I'm no good"* exists, the therapist needs to determine where that came from by allowing the client to re-experience the originating event, and not just to discuss the incident in a logical manner. The client will have logically analysed his memories, perhaps for years to no avail. What he now requires is an alternative way of understanding the situation.

If we consider the language systems as developed within NLP, we find that two models have been created, each with specific uses and each dovetailing into the other, combining perfectly to fulfil the language patterns of NLP.

The first set of language patterns was developed during the early 1970s and was derived from the ongoing study of certain therapists who were regularly using certain questions and language structures while working with their clients. This language pattern contained within it a level of precision, not normally found in everyday conversational language, and became known as the **Precision Model**, or the **Meta Model**. (Bandler & Grinder, 1975.) Its use enables you to drill down into the information being given to you by a client so that you can begin to question the specific issues that are underlying the deep structure of the actual problem he has.

The second language pattern that was developed became known as the **Milton Model**, named after Milton Erickson, and was in effect the exact opposite of the Precision Model. Its structure was developed in a way that meant the language would bypass the analytical part of the mind and be accepted by the unconscious mind without any interference or conscious intervention.

12.3 GOLD Counselling™ language patterns

The language used within GOLD Counselling™ has in itself been developed to enable the detailed analysis of individual beliefs to be carried out in a simple and accurate manner. In the same way that the Meta Model is very precise and the Milton Model is very vague, the GOLD Counselling™ language has been developed to be specifically vague.

Consider the different effects of the following questions on the client's problem.

Client: *I don't seem to be able to give up smoking*

Meta Model questions:

Therapist: *How do you know that you don't seem able to?*

        What else don't you seem able to do?

        What would happen if you did give up smoking?

Milton Model questions:

Therapist: *So, are there many things that you've not been able to give up?*

        It may be that you just don't give up for long enough?

        What's important for you in giving up smoking?

GOLD Counselling™ questions:

Therapist: *Where did I learn to believe the belief that I don't seem able to give up smoking?*

        What happened to me to lead me to believe the belief that I don't seem able to give up smoking?
        How did I learn to believe the belief that I don't seem able to give up smoking?

The Meta Model and the Milton Model will cause the client to look at his problem from a different perspective, but only GOLD Counselling™ questioning will direct the client back to the originating time when the belief was first installed.

An understanding of both the Meta Model and the Milton Model will significantly enhance your capabilities to work with GOLD Counselling™. This is because when working with the GOLD method you are presented on paper with the actual language which expresses the unconscious thoughts which your client believes all the time - his thoughts are fulfilling his beliefs. Each one in turn is being fulfilled - some for just an instant, some for longer periods of time. This cyclic nature is related to the amount of energy that the client is expending in fulfilling his beliefs. Further information about how energy is used with beliefs will be found in Chapter 7.

Let us take this as an example. Suppose that in a GOLD Counselling™ analysis to identify where someone first developed an inability to ask questions in public, one of the central thoughts was as follows:

"I'd always get told off, now."

This sentence reveals, not just a grammatical error, but in addition a deeply-held unconscious belief that he is still being told off, and this is linked to the current problem. Readers may notice that this is similar to the errors perpetrated by the unconscious mind which were documented by Sigmund Freud and later given the unofficial name "Freudian slips." This type of language was also developed and codified from the modelling of Milton Erickson and forms part of the ambiguity patterns, such as syntactic ambiguity and phonetic ambiguity. This closeness of language indicates that all patterns are being derived from the same sources deep within the unconscious mind.

13. How To Create A GOLD Counselling™ Topic List

13.1 Subject selection

In order to understand which thoughts your client holds as Primary Beliefs, he must first create a list which details all his thoughts about the chosen topic. This topic list should contain ALL of the beliefs, memories, and comments that come into his conscious mind when he considers the chosen topic. Some may be positive and others negative. Some may be clearly related and others, apparently unconnected.

It is essential that your client write down EVERY thought which comes into his mind. He must NOT consciously delete any. Furthermore, he must be instructed to write down all that he believes either all the time or sometimes and NOT what he wants to believe, or tries to believe. The latter types of beliefs are found within affirmations and positive thinking and its problematic influence will be elaborated on further in Chapter 16. Suffice it to say that we consider this type of thinking to be "Fools Gold" since what it apparently offers is, in effect, worthless.

> *"There is nothing worse than self-deception*
> *when the deceiver is always within us."*
>
> *Plato*

The thoughts which enter your client's conscious mind will be many and varied. Some will be words and others will be sentences. There may be feelings, sounds, sentences or whole paragraphs. In some cases the thoughts will be very symbolic, almost dream-like. Each and every one MUST be written down.

The topic for which a list is constructed will be based on a specific topic, such as *Happiness, Wealth, Stress* or *Pain*. The topic may have been selected either by the client although based on your understanding of the presenting symptoms or you will have selected a topic yourself.

From the information presented in the topic list we are then able to determine how the experiences of the client have led to the formation of specific beliefs. It is from these beliefs that his choices about how to carry on his life have been formed.

To enable you to understand the different types of subjects which could be used as a topic, we have listed below a few examples:

Example Topic Headings

I am/me	Friends
Work	Sexuality
Success	Illness
Happiness	Parents
Partners	Fear
Change	Relationships
Money	Feelings

Our experience with GOLD Counselling™ has revealed that it is a powerful analytical technique. We would, therefore, recommend that all prospective users start by working with the headings shown above. It is only once you have fully understood how the GOLD technique operates and have successfully worked through all the above topics that we would suggest you develop a GOLD™ Counselling analysis on other topics.

13.2 Writing the GOLD Counselling™ topic list

It is essential that your client is able to access the appropriate state while constructing his list. To do this you may need to show him how best to relax and focus his mind, perhaps with the use of simple relaxation techniques such as control of breathing. Alternatively for those of you with NLP knowledge, finger anchoring, New Behaviour Generator or a Circle of Excellence could be found to be useful to install in him the appropriate resources of previous memories when he experienced comfort or calmness thus creating the required state.

Once you have been able to allow him to access the required state, you should instruct him as follows:

1. to sit calmly and quietly in a place that is right for him in which it is unlikely that he will be disturbed

2. to write the chosen topic on the head of a piece of paper with only the topic as a header

3. to focus on the topic and as he focuses on the topic, to write in sequence down the paper, each and every thought that comes into his mind

4. to write whatever thoughts enter the mind, letting his unconscious mind dictate the path along which the thoughts move

5. to write down whatever the thought is

6. to allow no justification - whatever comes to mind is OK and should be noted down

7. to write down items even if they are not understood or are irrational or unexpected, without judgement

8. to write down items even if they appear to conflict with or contradict other items on the list

9. to ignore any apparent errors of grammar, punctuation or mixtures of past, present or future tense

10. to compile a list of between 10 to 30 items on the chosen topic

When preparing the list, each item should have a letter allocated in the left margin, starting with capital A. If the list exceeds 26 items, continue with AA, AB, AC and so on. Letters and not numbers should be used

Analysis has shown that the ideal length for a list is from 10 to 30 items. By suggesting to your client that he keeps his list short, this acts as a suggestion to his unconscious mind. The unconscious mind then presents the relevant information within a list of the appropriate size.

Once this list is prepared and a belief map has been created, you will often be presented with information which indicates where other work will be required to assist your client. This is because thoughts are not independent; all are inter-related. Therefore, in presenting information on a single topic, this topic may actually be related to another issue. This can be compared to a family tree, where all the individual levels and families are connected by ones before them back to the first family members.

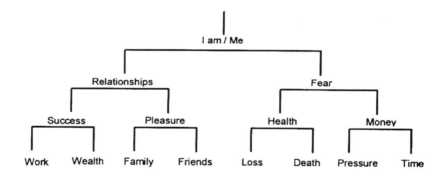

In order to enable you to begin to understand what a GOLD Counselling™ list would resemble when completed by a client, we have included an example of an actual list produced by a client on the topic of **"Relationships"**. This was produced following exactly the same instructions as those included in this chapter.

Topic: Relationships

A Grumpy

B Hard

C Take time

D Good sometimes

E Rough

F Crafty

G Enjoyable

H Never last

I Always problems

J Hidden agendas

K Love

L Not much love

M Difficult

13.3 Linking the items on the list

On completing the previous steps, you will now be presented with a list, generated with the full assistance of your client's unconscious mind which gives details of the main beliefs about the chosen topic. It might have been possible for your client to have continued the list further; some lists have comprised over one hundred items. However, by suggesting to the unconscious mind the desired length of the list, those items deemed most important will have surfaced.

The next step in the procedure is to ask your client to scan through each of the items on his list and, as if without any conscious thought, to connect all of these together.

When doing this, there are specific instructions which he should be given:

1. to let his unconscious mind do the process naturally

2. to recognise that no letter can link back to itself

3. to ensure that one item can only connect to one other item

4. to note that several items can all link to the same item

5. to emphasise that whatever way he feels he should connect the list is correct - there is no right or wrong way to connect each item

6. to ensure that there are no duplicated or similar words on the list

If, after completing the list, a word or phrase is found to have been duplicated, this should be challenged and your client should be instructed either to delete it or to replace it with a fresh item.

The example below shows how the belief list for the topic **"Relationships"** appeared once it was completed with each item on it linked correctly.

Topic: Relationships

A	Grumpy	M
B	Hard	M
C	Take time	G
D	Good sometimes	K
E	Rough	B
F	**Crafty**	I
G	Enjoyable	D
H	**Never last**	**K**
I	**Always problems**	**M**
J	Hidden agendas	F
K	**Love**	**H**
L	Not much love	F
M	**Difficult**	F

For this topic, "**Relationships**", the client can be seen to have two separate belief structures held for the one topic. One has Primary Beliefs of **H-K** and the other belief structure has Primary beliefs of **F-I-M**. This often occurs and is not an indication that the process has been completed incorrectly.

On the following page we have set out the format which should be used when carrying out a GOLD Counselling™ session. It is permitted to photocopy this, as many times as is required, or to prepare your own identical format.

The GOLD Counsellors Association™ topic list

TOPIC:

A ....

B ....

C ....

D ....

E ....

F ....

G ....

H ....

I ....

J ....

K ....

L ....

M ....

N ....

O ....

P ....

Q ....

R ....

S ....

T ....

U ....

V ....

13.4 Constructing the belief map

Once your client has created his list of items and identified to which item each is connected, it is then possible to construct a map of his belief structure.

This structure will, in a pictorial manner, set out exactly how each and every thought related to the selected topic is linked together. In doing so, it will also identify which beliefs are Primary Beliefs and which are Secondary Beliefs. To do this, one connects by arrows each of the related beliefs, ensuring that the arrow indicates the direction of flow of each belief from one to another. Once this belief map has been created it is possible to identify where problem areas exist and which beliefs are the Primary Beliefs - those which underpin the whole belief structure.

Once you have created this belief structure you can begin to understand exactly why the client has what he considers to be his "problem". In reality, it is his unconscious mind working artfully and simply to fulfil his beliefs.

The belief map below was created from the thoughts presented by the client for the topic **"Relationships"**.

TOPIC: Relationships

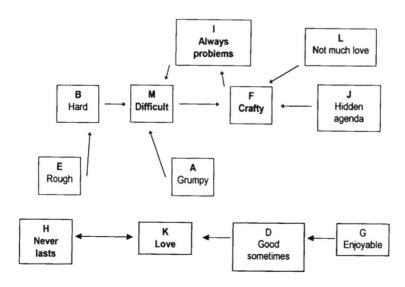

14. How Can Beliefs Be Changed?

14.1 Overview

As discussed in Chapter 3, so many people feel that once they've learnt to behave, do, or think in a certain way, it is impossible to change. Well, they are right. That feeling they have is in itself a belief. Unless that can be changed, they won't change. To change a belief, we first need to understand what we believe now and where this belief came from.

GOLD Counselling™ works because with it you can use the only approach which will facilitate permanent change. What needs to happen is that we trace the thoughts in the client's mind back to the source of the problem. Once there we are then able to identify the specific piece of false reasoning which persuaded him to believe that he should act or think in a certain way. You will always find corrupted information at the centre of any restricting or limiting beliefs. On correcting this corruption, either by removal or redesign, change will always occur.

When working with a client's beliefs, it is the client's belief system itself which must change in order for the desired change to happen.

The only way that this can happen is by your discovering what your client's beliefs are, NOW.

14.2 The difference between perception and belief

Our minds can only allow us to see what we believe and, therefore, we cannot see what we don't believe. Have you ever been in the situation whereby you have attempted unsuccessfully to convince someone that he is wrong? All the various arguments which you put up are discounted or ignored by him, often he will make your views seem small and his own ideas more important. It's as if he just can't or won't listen or see your point of view.

Perceptions are not facts, they are only a reflection of the beliefs of the perceiver. However, we all tend to believe our senses and assume that they are never wrong.

To test this we have included two exercises for you to carry out.

Exercise 1.

Read the following sentence out loud twice.

> THE FINISHED FILES ARE THE RESULT OF YEARS OF SCIENTIFIC EXPERIENCE COMBINED WITH THE EXPERIENCE OF MANY YEARS

Now, without reference to the written words, ask yourself how many letter **Fs** were there in the sentence?

Then check by reading the sentence from the page again.

The answer is six. Many people hear the F in "of" and *believe* it is a letter V. This is how the filtering of beliefs causes us to miss information without realising it.

Exercise 2.

Read the following sentence out loud

Now re-read it backwards and notice the error.

14.3 Belief identification

The actual symptoms of the client's beliefs are always present in the here and now. The client's unconscious mind has no shame in upholding his beliefs. This fact can be used by the therapist to bring about change in his belief structure since the unconscious mind is proud of its ability to remember exactly when a belief was formed.

It is possible to imagine the unconscious mind as the ultimate civil service department. A copy of everything is taken, just in case, and then filed and counter-filed. This means that when questioned in the correct way, the unconscious mind will release all the information asked of it, with delight. The unconscious mind has no concept of what a conscience is or what a conscience does. It doesn't care how or why a belief was formed, it only knows that it was formed, in the past, and still needs to be fulfilled.

When using GOLD Counselling™ the client is directed to return to the **exact time** when, and place where, the belief was formed. When the client has returned to that moment in time it is then possible to recreate the original feeling or emotion attached to that belief. The therapist can then dissect and analyse the memory with the client to ascertain both the actual event and his interpretation of it. A change must occur here for permanent change to take effect in the now.

It is from this position where the event and the interpretation can be separated that one is able to show the client how to re-evaluate, reappraise and then restructure that original belief through the creation of a fresh belief.

It will usually be the case that a client's beliefs will change daily and, in doing so, will often appear to conflict. Perhaps in the morning he may feel sad but by lunchtime he has moved into being relaxed and feels happier in the latter part of the afternoon. Most people would put this purely down to the situation they are in at present. However, once armed with an understanding of the **cyclic nature of beliefs**, a therapist will be able to understand how this change in emotions is natural and expected.

Of course, what we want to do for our client is to reduce the amount of time he spends in the less comfortable and more limiting emotional states and correspondingly to increase the amount of time he spends in rewarding states.

When working with a client, the method to enable him to focus on a particular part of the cycle is to ask the question *"What are you feeling right now?"*. This will encourage him to identify his beliefs and enable us to access his belief cycle. It is important to focus him on the NOW moment so that he can identify existing beliefs and not either old beliefs or future desires.

Once we have identified the originating belief, we can then focus the client on pinpointing where and how the belief was first learned. This concept reinforces the idea of the belief structure as a living organism - growing and connecting to new beliefs as time moves on. Therapy can then be applied to eliminate key areas where a negative influence is at work.

The therapist can be imagined as acting like a professional gardener who has been commissioned to reorganise and totally redesign a significantly overgrown garden. He would not waste time just tidying up the edges. No, he needs to quickly find the most powerful, most damaging weeds and plants and remove these, roots as well, so that they will no longer influence the way in which the garden grows ever again. And this is what the therapist can do with GOLD Counselling™ techniques.

14.4 Process Overview

GOLD Counselling™ techniques make it simple for the therapist to identify problem areas and to effect changes easily and without any detrimental effects on the client. This can be achieved by:

    identifying the appropriate place in the belief structure to attach the new belief

    installing the new belief using the least amount of energy required

New beliefs can be installed in the client's unconscious mind using various techniques because the unconscious mind will seek to find an answer to any and all questions, be they real or imagined. The therapist can restructure a belief using the following approaches:

    by posing a question to the client which encourages his own examination of his belief

    by the creation of a new belief

    via a positively-worded suggestion

    by encouraging the client to play with thoughts and ideas in his mind

    by exploring the semantics of exactly who did what, who said what and who was actually responsible for the experience

15. Identifying The Belief Source

15.1 Key points to remember when restructuring beliefs

The beliefs which your client has mapped out on the paper in front of you may have existed for many years. In addition, every thought will have a level of emotion attached, some weak, some extremely powerful. Furthermore, we must recognise that many of these beliefs may be extremely useful and empowering, but they have become attached to other negative and limiting beliefs. Therefore, before you attempt to restructure any beliefs, you should understand the following points about the process of carrying out belief restructuring:

it is important to correct any conflicting belief loops in your client's map of beliefs which may be causing confusion - although sometimes merely the revisitation of the memory causes the necessary change

always correct Primary Beliefs

always correct the most detrimental Primary Belief in a loop by evaluating its Secondary Beliefs

eliminate beliefs which are detrimental to the success of therapy first (e.g. failure or worthlessness)

the elimination of one belief will naturally explode the other or others related to it in the belief loop

ensure that the nub of the problem is correctly pinpointed before starting to restructure beliefs (i.e. change the problem, not the symptom)

recognise the significance of saturating the unconscious mind with the existing belief - the client must be totally absorbed in the question

check to see if there are other beliefs supporting the original as a belief may be learned on more than one occasion

always bear in mind the fact that nature hates vacuums and it is, therefore, important to reconstruct and/or fill the gap created by the review of beliefs

conversely, the mind may appear to lose unimportant memories when there is no high emotional content contained within the belief cell

consider carefully the links between major complexes before starting to restructure beliefs in order to be able to see the complete picture

when dealing with a complex of highly-sensitive material, start by restructuring the least serious belief first in terms of emotional content

be sensitive to potentially high-anxiety material in your client's lists (e.g. items such as 'fear' and the name of a family member closely connected may indicate repressions of child abuse)

recognise that a client may unconsciously be resisting or avoiding change

look for ways in which a client links items on the list so as to ensure absolute free association of ideas (i.e. check for logical connections indicating that this is what he wants to believe or feels he should believe)

ensure that a client creates a list of beliefs in the present tense in order to capture **NOW** moment beliefs

Provided that the therapist is mindful of these points he will be able to assist the client in locating the central core of the beliefs which underpin his problem. This will be direct and accurate and will ignore any peripheral issues surrounding the problem, and any erroneous associations or memories which the client falsely believes are the originating causes.

15.2 Belief restructuring techniques

The GOLD Counselling™ techniques contained herein will enable a therapist to assist clients to correct a limiting or inappropriate belief and install a positive belief in its place.   This is achievable by taking your client through the following process:

1.   Enter a state of rapport with your client, directing him to relax himself and let go of any tensions he may have - mental or physical.

2. Facilitate in him simple breathing techniques so as to allow him to focus on his internal experiences.

3. Ask your client to repeat to himself in the first person the selected question.

4. Ask him to repeat the question again and again, altering your voice tone and inflection with the prime objective of flooding and tiring his unconscious mind with the question.

5. Ask him to identify when, where and how the belief was first formed.

6. Regress your client to that specific point in his life when the existing belief was first formed.

7. Establish that the belief was formed at an earlier or inappropriate time in your client's life.

8. Verify that the belief was formed for the wrong reasons (e.g. a belief held erroneously by an authority figure).

9. Ask your client to identify and experience subsequent events whose outcomes had been shaped by the earlier belief.

10. Ask your client to acknowledge now that the negative belief is no longer necessary, feasible or appropriate.

11. Ask your client to imagine how the future would be if the new belief were installed.

There will be certain circumstances in which more complex belief-restructuring techniques will be required. These techniques include:

1. developing new beliefs for a client who has no previous blueprint in his earlier life with which to form a positive belief - the new belief will need to be installed and fixed to an existing belief and then tested

2. dealing with complex beliefs which form a large loop

3. working with a client who has a number of belief complexes and each of these is inter-related.

15.3 The need to tire the mind

The unconscious mind has within it the information we need to locate where and when a belief was first formed. However, it may be unwilling to present this information to us. First we must tire it, through focusing the whole of the mind on one particular issue. By repeating again and again the particular belief, posed as a question, the unconscious mind will be forced to flow back in time to the originating place. Without this tiring effect, the mind will either present a recent incident, one of the Secondary Beliefs, or even produce something unrelated, acting as a screen for the original event. It is only through tiring the mind that we can quickly ascertain the originating cause of the belief. The ego protects beliefs so it is the ego that needs to be commanded to reveal the source of the belief. This it can also do without any resistance if the process is explained correctly.

15.4 Finding the belief source

Before a therapist carries out a GOLD Counselling™ analysis, he must ensure that he prepares a thorough case history of the client. This is to ensure that he can determine whether the symptom being presented can be worked on initially or whether there is a deeper issue which should be addressed first. For example, if the client has had a history of visiting various therapists, all unsuccessful, an analysis of the beliefs surrounding **"Failure"** would be an essential first step, to eliminate the secondary gain currently being fulfilled.

Once the belief structure map has been created, your next objective will be to determine which of the thoughts within the structure need to be revised so that new learnings and understandings can take place.

When obtaining your client's focus on his beliefs, it is essential that your language is precise. Where possible always use the first person singular (e.g. *"Where did I learn to believe the belief that I ...?"*) and, where possible, always use exactly the same words as those appearing on the GOLD Counselling™ topic list. Your objective will be to saturate your client's mind, to the total exclusion of everything else, with his existing belief and ask him to follow you in repeating the specific question again and again in his own mind in order to ensure that the precise source is identified.

A typical way of preparing your client to identify a limiting or inappropriate belief might be to begin by saying to him (while keeping rapport):

Therapist: *And as you relax there ... calm and relaxed ...just allow your body now ... to discover that place of comfort there ... inviting those arms and legs ... those hands and feet ... to release those tensions now ... and you can be proud of your mind ... constantly fulfilling all your beliefs ... never questioning ... just doing ... only obeying ... your faithful servant ... and perhaps now you may want to know when and where you learned to believe that you believe that ...*

Depending on the actual belief which your client needs to focus on, one of the phrases, such as those listed below, would be appropriate:

Where/when/how did I learn to believe the belief Relationships, bad?

Where/when/how did I learn to believe that I believe ..

Where/when/how did I learn to believe the belief ...

Where/when/how did I learn the belief that I believe ...

Where/when/how did I learn that I believe ...

Let your mind take you to that time, that place where I first learned to believe that I believe ...

Where/when/how did I learn to believe the belief leg pain, loneliness?

When did I learn to believe that I was (ability/feeling) in (situation) ...

When directing your client to consume his mind with this question, the client should adopt a relaxed pose, sitting or lying down and with his eyes closed. Some clients, however, will not feel comfortable closing their eyes. In these situations, simply pose the following question:

What do you see yourself doing? Tell me about that learning.

In many cases, a therapist will find that just the act of posing the question will provoke a profound emotional reaction within the client. (This is known as an *abreaction*). This abreaction may take as many different forms as there are different ways to experience something emotionally. This could include tears, shouting, body shaking or coldness.

15.5 Multiple-learning points

As discussed previously, the objective of GOLD Counselling™ is to take the client back to the original memory so that he can understand what the specific learning was back then. Normally there will be one profound learning from a single memory but there will sometimes be instances where the experience was so profound that two or more beliefs were created from it.

This means that the client will have this memory in more than one belief structure. At the time of the incident, the intensity of emotions which were released (or possibly are still repressed) caused the mind, in effect, to create multiple copies of the memory and to record them in different belief structures.

This is the reason why, if you were to take a client through a sequence of GOLD Counselling™ sessions, memories that had been discharged from earlier topics may appear in later ones. This does not mean your previous sessions were unsuccessful; it only means you have now unearthed a multiple-learning point.

For example, a boy was scolded and kept in after producing school results below the expectations of his parents. The two beliefs which he formed from this event were *"I am stupid"* and *"I am no good"*. Your client would benefit from reorganising both of these limiting beliefs. However, unless both appeared in one map you would not realise that the same incident was supporting two or more beliefs.

15.6 Cumulative-learning points

When asked to focus his mind back to the specific time when he first learnt to believe the belief, most clients will be able to locate the appropriate memory. However, in some instances, a client will respond that there is no specific memory, more a feeling of knowing this - the belief having been built up over a long time. We would always recommend that, as the therapist, you should aim to uncover the originating cause and since your client's unconscious mind has hidden away the original memory for a long time, you may need to push forcefully to enable it to reveal the truth. This is why the approach of tiring the mind through repeatedly asking it the same question is essential.

If your client still suggests that there is no particular time incident, stop the session. Ask him there and then whether he really does or whether he really does not want to learn when and where he learnt to believe the belief. Be forceful and assertive. Accept that your client would probably rather keep his problem instead of realising where it came from. Once this is realised, however, he will see the situation from a different and liberating perspective.

However, in situations where the client really cannot identify an originating memory, it is quite acceptable to work with the feeling that is being experienced by the client. The success of GOLD Counselling™ is in no way undermined by this occurrence. It is rather that the benefits to the client would be more profound if the original memory were revealed since we can then correct the exact incident, rather than purely the feeling based on his interpretations of the incidence.

16. Eliminating Negative Beliefs

16.1 Methodology

Once you have facilitated in the client an understanding of where he first learnt his belief, you have already carried out a significant piece of change-work. However, the process is not complete until the old belief no longer exerts any influence over the client.

At this stage your client will usually be in an altered state of awareness, very inwardly focused and extremely sensitive and suggestible to whatever you say. It is extremely important that you stay in rapport with your client, keeping him relaxed. Focus on using the specific words of your client, as identified on the GOLD Counselling™ topic list.

From this position the therapist must now determine how the belief became accepted as true by the client. This could have occurred in a variety of ways. To assist, we have detailed some examples below.

16.2 A belief formed by observation

Let us take as an example a client who is having relationship problems and has discovered that his Primary Belief was formed by watching his parents behave in a particularly argumentative way.

Therapist: *So if I am hearing you right, I am hearing you say that your mother and your father are fighting in the living room, then?*

Client: *Yes*

Therapist: *So if I am hearing you right, what I am hearing you say is that you believe your parents believe that their marriage means arguments ... then?*

Client: *(Pause, considering different viewpoint) Yes.*

Therapist: *So on that day, in that living room, back then...*

16.3 A belief formed by being told

In this instance, the GOLD Counselling™ topic sheet revealed that the client's Primary Belief was that he was told by another person *"I think I am stupid."*

Therapist: So if I am hearing you right, Mr XX, your school teacher is saying that he believes you are stupid, then?"

Client: Yes

Therapist: So if I am hearing you right, what I am hearing you say is that you believe that Mr X believes that you are stupid, then?

Client: (Pause, cognitive review of information) Yes

Therapist: So on that day, in that classroom, back then ...

16.4 A belief formed by self-perception

For this client the GOLD Counselling™ topic list revealed that his Primary Belief was formed by self-perception and was *"I'm not a good person, I let people down."*

Therapist: So if I am hearing you right, I am hearing you say that you believe that on that day, at that time, when you were seven years old, you didn't stick up for your friend in the classroom?

Client: Yes

Therapist: So if I am hearing you right, what I am hearing you say is that your friend didn't think that you stuck up for your friend, back then?

Client: (Pause, recognising difference) Yes

Therapist: So on that day, when you were in that classroom, you believed that your friend believed ...

17. Restructuring The Remaining Positive Beliefs

17.1 Overview

As discussed in Chapter 10, the unconscious mind will fulfil both positive and negative beliefs without question. *"I'm a failure"* and *"I'm successful"* are both appropriate and congruent beliefs within the unconscious mind, provided that it has stored away reference experiences to back these up.

While no-one would disagree that removal of the first belief would be beneficial, if the belief "I'm successful", were connected to "I'm a failure" after GOLD counselling the removal of one belief would inevitably result in the loss of the other.

When reviewing a GOLD Counselling™ topic list, you will usually identify that positive beliefs are attached to negative beliefs. Following the elimination of the central negative belief, any useful beliefs attached to negative arms of the belief structure would slowly fade away.

What needs to happen in these cases is that the free-floating positive beliefs are then attached to the reset positive beliefs so as to form an even stronger reinforcement to the newly-formed attitude of mind.

17.2 The process of bridging beliefs

We must allow the client to consider the old negative belief in a way which permits his unconscious mind to construct a fresh, positive and liberating belief. Once this has occurred, his unconscious mind will reformat the belief structure into a totally different pattern. This structure will then exclude the previously-limiting Primary Beliefs and the connected, limiting Secondary Beliefs.

So that your client can accept the newly-formed beliefs, a therapist might ask a question phrased as follows:

What would there have to be in your mind, now, for you to believe that you believe that ...

What would you need to believe in order to believe ...
What would need to happen for me to believe that I believe that I ...

... now, allow your unconscious mind to show you the effects of today's experience on the rest of your days from now ...

If we work through the following example we can understand how this principle would be applied in practice. The client has produced a GOLD Counselling™ list on the topic **"Relationships"**.

Topic: Relationships

A Happy		C
B Sad		**H**
C Good		G
D Bad		B
E Restricting		G
F Fun		A
G Manipulating		B
H Lonely		**B**

Naturally, we will want to revise the limiting Primary Beliefs **B** *Sad* and **H** *Lonely*. Let us assume that this has now occurred. Unless we bridge the positive beliefs **A** *Happy*, **C** *Good* and **F** *Fun*, these will no longer be beliefs held in respect of relationships. To do this, we can pose the following style of question:

What do you need to believe to believe the belief Relationships, Good?

In answering this question your client will then have connected the belief to the new structure which was formed from the revision of the old, limiting Primary Belief.

The appropriate question can be identified by referring to the map produced from this topic list.

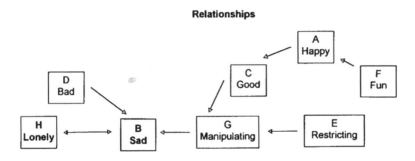

Relationships

17.3 Overnight integration

During our sleep, significant work is carried out by the unconscious mind in collating and sorting information based on our experiences of the previous day. Our mind always needs to connect new learnings to old experiences, only ever revising old experiences if forced to. It is, therefore, essential that any restructuring is completed on the same day, or else the memories within your client's mind will change and will no longer support the beliefs as written on the belief map. This means that any work carried out at a later session based on the old map would not be as effective, since the thoughts and beliefs will have already been restructured.

18. Future Pacing

With GOLD Counselling™ you must first confirm, using the client's language exactly, what it was he learnt to believe and from whom, where and when. Once the client has confirmed this, the therapist can then focus the client's mind on who it was that had, therefore, really held the belief in the past.

Once the client understands that the belief he believed was actually someone else's, a significant rearrangement in his belief structure will take place.

At this stage it is then appropriate to ask the client to review how this original incorrect learning has affected him since the originating time and up until the here and now. One method would be to suggest to him the following:

And you can allow your unconscious mind to start to show you the effects of that incident, there, then, on the rest of your life, up to now, as I count from 10 down to 1 ... 10 ... 9 ... 8 ... 7 ... 6 ... 5 ... 4 ... 3 ... 2 ... 1 ... that's right.

Provided that the therapist is calibrating all the time and noticing sensory feedback, he will recognise when the client has taken on the new belief. If the client stays quiet and appears to be processing internally, it is appropriate (after pausing for a short while) to ask what it is he is thinking. This will enable you to ensure that he is incorporating the new belief in the most useful way.

Often a client will find that once he has released the feelings associated with the original experience, he will gain insight into why subsequent events occurred in his life. This pattern can now stop.

19. Follow-Up

If a client were to undergo a subsequent GOLD Counselling™ analysis approximately three to four weeks after the original analysis had been worked through, it would be possible to determine whether other, previously-uncovered issues are now revealing themselves. We have always found that, provided the central belief core has been eliminated correctly, this follow-up map will always be structured significantly differently, with many of the old issues having just faded away and being no longer of any consequence whatsoever.

While this approach is very useful for a therapist undergoing his training so that he can recognise, first hand, how powerful the GOLD Counselling™ approach is at permanently removing limiting beliefs, we would not recommend carrying this out with a client unless he specifically requested a follow-up session. You should not need to prove that this technique works; it should be sufficient for you to know you are right and that the technique does work. After all, the change is natural and will come, whether the client notices it or not.

Section Three:

GOLD Counselling™
Case Studies

Introduction to Section Three

Section Three contains a selection of examples showing how GOLD Counselling™ has been used to facilitate change in clients. As you work through the examples you will notice that the complexity increases. You will find that, in some cases, additional topics have had to be prepared before the presenting problems could be worked through. In every case, however, the same approach, the same language and the same technique has been applied.

20. Case Studies

20.1 Overview of case studies

Let us suppose that your client has produced a list under the topic heading of **"I am"**. When asked to go back to locate the Primary Belief, the client speaks of the time when he had been falsely accused of stealing money and had received a reprimand from his mother. A way of questioning your client from this position would be:

"Where did you first learn to believe that you are guilty?"

On consideration of this question the client identified that the money had been given to him by his grandmother. From this position you would encourage your client to discover who should have accepted the label of being guilty in that situation. Your next question could be:

"So what I am hearing you say is that it was your mother who was guilty of accusing you falsely?"

Let your client focus his mind on this question. Let the understanding of the difference between what he had previously believed and what this question is inferring. Once the client has accepted the question and answered it positively, you should reinforce and augment the belief by asking the client to repeat with his internal voice statements such as:

"I believe my mother should feel guilty for making a false accusation."
or
"I believe my mother is guilty of falsely accusing me."

Once the client has resolved this individual learning about being guilty, it would be appropriate to identify whether there are additional experiences in his life coded as being guilty.

In order to ascertain where he may be, the client could now ask himself:

"... and where else did I learn to believe that I am guilty?"

As you review the case studies, we recommend that you construct a belief map for each one. In this way, you will be able to follow more closely the approach used by the therapist to facilitate change in the client.

20.2 Exam nerves case study

In this case study a client presented himself for treatment to help reduce or eliminate examination nerves.

Topic: Exam Nerves

A   I get it wrong

B   I can't focus

C   I know I'm a good student

D   I'm interested in the subject

E   I get nervous

F   People stare

G   I study hard

H   I have to get it right

I   People depend on me getting it right

J   I feel stupid

K   Confusing

L   I know the answers

Once the client had created the above list, he was asked to link the items and the result was as follows:

A	I get it wrong	L
B	I can't focus	C
C	I know I'm a good student	K
D	I'm interested in the subject	G
E	I get nervous	A
F	People stare	A
G	I study hard	D
H	I have to get it right	E
I	People depend on me getting it right	A
J	I feel stupid	A
K	Confusing	L
L	I know the answers	J

If you review this list you will notice from the collection of thoughts about the topic of examinations that the client has certain opposing beliefs. This is not unusual and would be expected, as indicated by the pre-suppositions of GOLD Counselling™ (refer back to Chapter 10 for further clarification).

We are not asking him to justify why he thinks what he thinks. We have no need for comments such as *"... and I feel stupid because I know I should be able to get it right."* All that is required is a list of his thoughts about the selected topic.

From the previous list of thoughts the client had written, the items have been linked together as set out below. You will notice that there are two sets of beliefs which are functioning in order to support this topic. These are held in place by two separate Primary Belief structures, **A-L-J** and **D-G**. Of these, the first structure is the one containing the negative beliefs and if you look at the number of supporting Secondary Beliefs around this structure, you will recognise that most of the client's energy will be expended in supporting beliefs **A** then **L**.

A I get it wrong	**L**
B I can't focus	C
C I know I'm a good student	K
D I'm interested in the subject	**G**
E I get nervous	A
F People stare	A
G I study hard	**D**
H I have to get it right	E
I People depend on me getting it right	A
J I feel stupid	**A**
K Confusing	L
L I know the answers	**J**

This can be expressed using the GOLD Counselling™ mappIng technique in a pictorial format.

Exams Nerves

Once we have this framework we then move on to ask the client about his belief in a very precise and specific way.

Therapist: *So you believe that you get it wrong?*

Client: *Yes.*

Therapist: *As you relax there ... your conscious mind still and quiet ... you may take some time now ... remembering that we spoke about ... learning ... how we learn to believe; and that you could, right now ... take the time necessary to help yourself discover something about ... your beliefs. Perhaps it is something that your unconscious mind .. can shed some light on ... a particular belief ... and I know that your unconscious mind is always proud of its ability to fulfil your beliefs. Proud of its ability to show you all the necessary information ... including where you first learned that belief ... "Exam Nerves, I get it wrong." That's right ... just hold that thought in your mind ... Just think "Where did I learn to believe that I believe Exam Nerves, I get it wrong?" and wait ... and in a moment your unconscious mind will show you where it first learned to believe "Exam Nerves, I get it wrong."*

The client then found himself remembering a particular time when he was in a classroom at school. There was a competition in which the class had been divided into two groups. The teacher was playing a type of quiz game and the students were required to answer a general question. The client remembered that one particular question was asked and no-one on the client's side knew the answer. The teacher had put pressure on the client to answer the question and so finally, under pressure, he gave an answer that someone else had shouted out before ... and it was wrong.

Getting this wrong cost his team the game and because of this he was abused and made to feel terrible by the other students. The client remembered feeling stupid, and then how the others were saying things like *"You always get it wrong."* The ironic thing about all this was that the client had indeed known the correct answer.

However, the problem seemed to stem from the fact that, at that moment, the client was so humiliated that things were never the same again. His classmates continued to tease him for much of the remainder of the term.

The flow of questioning at this point proceeded as follows:

Therapist: *If I heard you right, you believe that you get it wrong?*

Client: *Yes.*

Therapist: *So what you mean is that on that day, at that time, in that class-room, with that question?*

Client: *Yes.*

Therapist: *So there are other times when you got it right in a test?*

Client: *(A slower, deeper, considered answer) Yes.*

Therapist: *So when you look back to that time in the classroom then ... you got it wrong then?*

Client: *Yes.*

Therapist: *So what do you mean about you **always** get it wrong?*

Client: *Well, I don't always get it wrong.*

Therapist: *So what is it that you believe?*

Client: *I see ... well I believe that sometimes I get it wrong and sometimes I get it right.*

From this position the therapy continued dealing with other issues, this one having been resolved.

20.3 Public speaking case study

The client was a 26 year-old male lawyer who was in his final year at law school when attending our practice. He had a serious problem with public speaking and with his self-esteem. This affected him so much that although he was deaf in one ear he would not wear a hearing aid for fear of people noticing this and laughing at him.

Topic: Public speaking

A	**Everyone should be able to do it without worry**	**B**
B	**I can't do it, obviously**	**A**
C	Public speaking does not have to be serious	D
D	If you make a mess of it, it's not a question of life or death	E
E	But I feel for me it is a question of life or death	B
F	Public speaking is something that should be enjoyed	G
G	I personally hate it enormously	E
H	**Public speaking should be used to advance a person's career**	**I**
I	**My career will go backwards if I can't master it**	**H**
J	Public speaking is an opportunity to express one's views or feelings	H
K	Public speaking should not frighten a person	A
L	I feel stupid	K
M	Public speaking should not give a person sleepless nights	K
N	But I get sleepless nights before my speeches	M
O	Good public speakers can make a lot of money by persuasion in their arguments	H
P	Public speech should make the audience listen	O
Q	I feel I bore them	P

Within this belief map there was found to be two sets of Primary Beliefs, **A-B** and **H-I** as set out in the belief map.

Public speaking

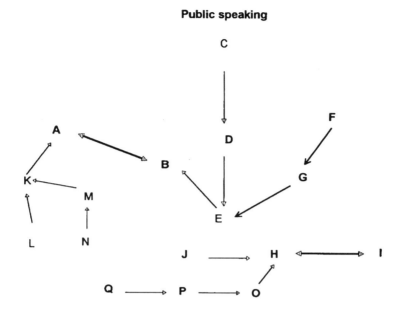

Once this had been ascertained, we asked our client to relax and make himself comfortable so that he could begin focusing on his unconscious mind. The questioning then took the following path:

Therapist: *... and ask yourself, where did I learn to believe the belief Public Speaking, I can't do it, obviously?*

Client: *My Dad.*

Therapist: *Tell me about it.*

Client: *I'm four years old and in the front room trying to build a Lego wall. Dad is there. He keeps saying "You can't do it. I'm telling you, you can't do it." I go to the kitchen to ask my mother to help me but she is too busy. She is cooking and looking after my baby sister. She says "Ask your father to help you." But I know he will just say, "I told you, you can't do it."*

Therapist: *So, your father believed then that you could not build that Lego wall. Is that right?*

Client: *I don't know. It was his way of challenging us to make us do better. He thought that if he challenged us we would try even harder and then be able to do things.*

Therapist: *But it didn't work that time, did it?*

Client: *No. It made me believe that I could not do it.*

Therapist: *So am I right in saying that your father gave you this mistaken belief?*

Client: *Yes, but he did not do it to harm me.*

Therapist: *That's right. But it did harm you. Don't you think it's time you gave that belief back to where and who it came from, back to your father?*

Client: *Yes.*

The next steps in the session consisted of our client's visualisation of that scene once again, but this time he saw himself wearing a sash that was much too big and baggy for him with the wording "I can't do it" on it. He then visualised putting the sash around his father whom it fitted perfectly.

Therapist: *How does that feel?*

Client: *It feels good. I know that I can do it, I can do anything I try to do, I guess I've always known that really but there was a part of me that believed differently.*

Therapist: *And now.*

Client: *Now I know I can - that the belief is gone.*

An interesting post-script to this GOLD Counselling™ analysis was that the client and his partner turned up at our practice four months later. He had passed his final examinations and had received a good job offer. A major part of the examination was a presentation to the lecturer, the class and external examiners in which he was required to argue a case which he had been assigned.

20.4 Weight control case study

Barbara was a 50-year-old nurse who had been battling with weight problems for years, ever since her divorce at 26 from an abusive policeman. She remarried at 29 and seemed very happy. She told us she loved crusty white bread and that this was her biggest downfall.

Topic: Food

A I enjoy food		C
B Food is healthy		C
C Food makes me fat		E
D **Eating food can comfort**		E
E **When I see food I have to eat it**		D
F Food can kill		A
G I enjoy feeding other people		B

Within this belief structure, the Primary Beliefs were focused at the connections of **D-E.**

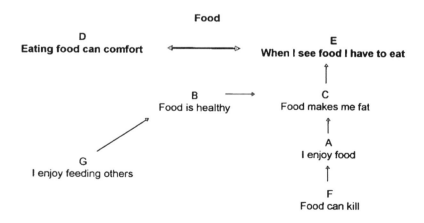

We then asked Barbara to close her eyes and relax using a very simple breathing exercise.

Therapist:	Where did I learn to believe the belief that when I see food I have to eat it?
Client:	I don't know. I can see a man's face. I know him but I'm not sure who he is.

Therapist:	Allow yourself to drift backwards in time until you recognise the man.
Client:	I don't know, I just know I know him.

Therapist:	You may have to go way back, perhaps to your early childhood even to find him.
Client:	He's a friend of my brother's. God. I haven't seen him in years.

Therapist:	Tell me, when did you first meet your brother's friend?
Client:	They were at school together. I remember him having dinner with us at Gran's.

Therapist:	Tell me about dinner at Gran's.
Client:	(Pause, now with tears rolling down her face) The whole family was always there for Sunday dinner and many times our friends were there as well. We used to eat in the kitchen. Gran had a really big old oak table and we would all sit down at the table. It was really nice, we'd talk about all sorts of things and the atmosphere was always lovely in Gran's kitchen. I remember there was always a basket of crusty rolls in the middle of the table, whenever we went there. Sometimes us children would go there during the week and Gran would look after us. She was always cooking or baking so we were usually in the kitchen.

Therapist:	Imagine yourself there in that kitchen now and tell me how it feels.
Client:	It's really nice and comfortable and it feels safe. Gran was always there if we wanted her.

Therapist:	Describe the kitchen.

Barbara proceeded to do so in great detail including the basket of crusty rolls that was always on the table and Gran making the children rolls whenever they felt hungry or needed cheering up. She still had tears pouring down her face while explaining this.

Therapist: So what do those crusty bread rolls mean to you?

Client: Comfort and security.

The next step in the GOLD Counselling™ analysis session was to carry out repair work with Barbara. She visualised the kitchen with a vase of flowers on the table replacing the bread rolls. Barbara has since lost about two stone and has joined a health and fitness club where she is doing very well.

20.5 Arachnophobia case study

This woman was in her 30s. When asked how long she had been a phobic, she replied that it was as long as she could remember, so the topic chosen was **"Spiders"**.

Topic: Spiders

A	Hairy	M
B	Dark	N
C	Big	F
D	Ugly	T
E	Fat	A
F	Beastly	G
G	Scary	H
H	Frightening	P
I	Sick in stomach	T
J	Scream	W
K	Shaky	O
L	**Spooky**	**V**
M	Creepy	V
N	Dark corners	V
O	Twitchy/nervous/edgy	W
P	**Fast**	**W**
Q	Threatening	G
R	**Pathetic**	**Y**
S	Non-threatening	Y
T	Revolting	M

U Spasmo	J
V Lurking	**L**
W Surprise	**P**
X Pretty (small ones)	S
Y Sad little creatures	**R**
Z Hideous	I
AA Extreme revulsion	Z
AB Shock/fright	J
AC Relief (when dead) but then again there's always another one somewhere	Z

As discussed previously, some beliefs which are identified will be useful and, as a therapist, you should act to keep these active. The Primary Belief structure **R-Y** is just such an example. In consequence, work was focused on the structure **P-W**, and specifically **"Fast"**.

Spiders

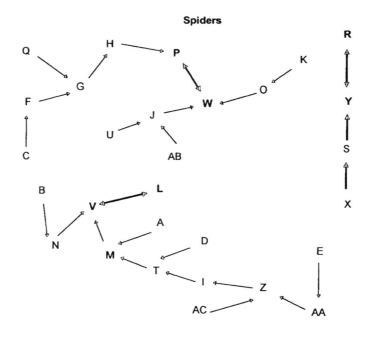

The client was then asked the question *"Where did I learn to believe the belief spider is fast?"*. This question was repeated and repeated and from this her unconscious mind led her to remembering being on the toilet next to the sink. Next she recollected seeing a spider appear from the sink and immediately abreacted with a scream. We then replayed the original scene to its conclusion and she was then able to see that the spider had been frightened itself and had run away.

When she returned for her next visit and was asked about spiders she replied, *"Well to be honest, I haven't noticed any."*

20.6 Self-sabotage case study

This client had a problem with generating more income and felt he never had enough money.

Money

A	It is difficult to get in large amounts	C
B	It is energy	C
C	Absolute belief will manifest any amount	D
D	**Money is unspiritual**	F
E	Having achieved a fortune leaves a career vacuum	B
F	**Having a fortune may cut me off from any further necessary development**	D
G	Can be dangerous in large amounts (personal attack etc.) *	
H	Can provide opportunities to explore personal development *	
I	Can provide the means to spread the word *	

Money

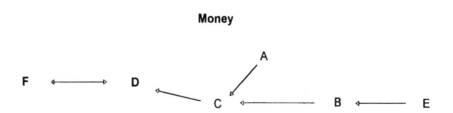

This brief list revealed the Primary Belief structure of **D-F**. Working on the belief *"Money is unspiritual"* took the client back to being in a class-room in Australia when he was 12. He remembered hearing his scripture teacher saying *"It is harder for a rich man to enter the kingdom of heaven than for a camel to pass through the eye of a needle"*. The client observed that although the teacher believed she was right, she was, in fact, in error. The client knew that many rich men do wonderful works with their money; work that would be impossible without it. The client was then able to revise this incorrect and limiting belief to *"Money is a spiritual neutral"*.

In addition the belief *"Having a fortune leaves a career vacuum"* has now been changed to *"Having achieved a fortune will help me expand my personal development."*

* The last three beliefs were not included in the analysis map. These were used to develop a separate map, unrelated to this case study. However, this list shows how one topic will often reveal other relevant information which will need to be treated separately (see Chapter 13.2 for further information).

20.7 Anger case study

Stuart is a 43-year-old management consultant. During the course of his sessions it had become apparent that he had suppressed a lot of anger.

Topic: Anger

A	Pure	B
B	I have a right to be angry	G
C	**You have no right to trample on me**	**D**
D	**I have rights**	**G**
E	Why can't things be perfect	L
F	Recognise I'm OK	G
G	**I matter**	**C**
H	You have no right to try to hurt me	K
I	I do not hurt people	H
J	Get things done	K
K	How dare you	C
L	I expect to be treated as an equal	C

Anger

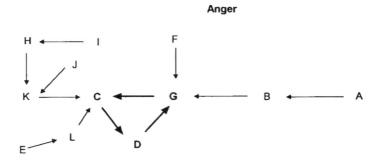

The theme within Stuart's list was of anger focused at one person. The Primary Belief structure of **C-D-G** bore this out. In addition, three specific issues kept on appearing during previous sessions:

> Being stuck
> Getting to the edge and then drawing back
> Anger at his father for allowing his grandmother to dominate the family

When he went back in his mind to his childhood he would easily slip into third position, adopt an observatory role and repeat verbatim what was being said to him. His memories were infused with a strong symbolic content.

Therapist: *Focus on that angry feeling, really feel that anger ... intensify it. Think about HOW DARE YOU! (feeding back his exact words to describe the feeling). Now tell me where did I learn to believe the belief I have been trampled on, that someone has tried to hurt me?*

Client: *She's very angry with me now. I'm telling you after all she's done for me, ungrateful, she's fuming, like a dragon breathing fire, like a witch going to do things to me. Mum's crying, she's frightened, doesn't want any harm to come to me, begging my Gran not to hurt me. "Please don't Mum, leave him alone". I'm not afraid. God she's going crazy, like a malevolent devil, she's so angry. How dare I. Revenge, she's going to have revenge, scary. My Dad's just looking over, he's not taking any part at all. Mum's so upset. I'm calm, don't dislike her, need to know, understand why she did it. God she's angry.*

Therapist: *Why she did what, Stuart?*

Client: *Malicious, horrible to my Dad. I can see her now a frail old lady. Very bitter about her husband being taken from her, alone. My dad, it's not his fault. She's so spiteful in her anger. I'm running around like an animal being chained to something, trying to get away, screaming, scared she's going to get me back for this, for talking about it now, after all she's done, taking my Dad in when he had no home.*

His comments continued in this way for a further ten minutes. Then we passed Stuart our punch pillow and we spent the remainder of the session facilitating in him the release of the anger he had held on to. After the session he said that before then he had never remembered his Gran becoming angry like that and that while in the session he was afraid that she was going to take her revenge on him for speaking out. She had actually died when he was 12.

Once this release had occurred, Stuart was able to understand where his trait of *"getting to the edge and then backing away"* had come from. At our next session he was much calmer and more relaxed.

20.8 Me case study

While there are various specific GOLD Counselling™ topics which we have identified as appropriate for use with clients, a standard topic we use with clients is "Me", This can be used to reveal issues relating to poor self-image or similar limitations. We would not apply this at the first session, but possibly by session three. This case study which follows was focused on this heading.

Kioto is a Japanese woman aged 45. She works as a PA to the director of a large Japanese company, one that is very tradition-bound. Kioto was an only child brought up by her parents in Japan, then when she was in her mid-twenties she came to England. Her father was a dentist, a gambler, a drug-addict and an alcoholic. Her mother committed the cardinal sin of taking a lover who followed the family every time they were forced to move by her father's behaviour at work. The family set success by academic achievement, particularly scientific. However, Kioto is creative rather than scientifically-oriented

Topic: Me

A	I was not loved by my parents	B
B	I lack a good model of a happy life	C
C	I could have achieved more if my childhood was not hampered by family problems	A
D	I don't know how to love unconditionally	L
E	I'm more flirtatious thank I want others to think	L
F	I have to work really hard to make a living	G
G	My life will always be hard	F
H	I'm very materialistic	L
I	I'm fairly snobbish	R
J	I am artistic	U
K	I am stingy but I pretend not to be	H

L I am selfish but this seems to be the only way to survive	**H**
M I am a victim of circumstances	A
N There is a part of me that has not grown properly	A
O I cannot be relied on	L
P If I finally conclude that my life will not work out, then I can kill myself	B
Q My enemy is myself	P
R I need to keep a good appearance and not to show my real self to outside	**I**
S I need to be very conscious of what others will think of me	I
T There is a new me which is struggling to come out	A
U I am stubborn	L

Me

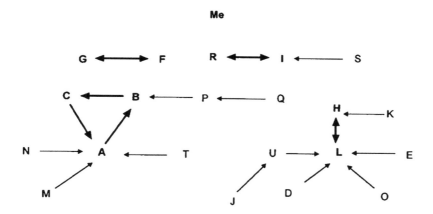

This list was structured around the following Primary Beliefs: C-A-B, G-F, H-L and I-R. Having reviewed the list, we asked Kioto to focus on a specific question and the following then occurred:

Therapist: *Where did I first learn to believe the belief I am selfish?*

Client: *I caused my father to lose face in front of visitors.*

Therapist: *Tell me about it.*

Client: *I was little, only about maybe two or three, and I was, I don't know, making a noise or trying to get his attention or something and my father had to shout at me in front of his visitors. After, when they were gone, he told me what a bad girl I was, how I made him lose face.*

Therapist: *So where did I learn to believe that I believe I am selfish?*

Client: *Well, I taught myself, because if I was being bad and causing my father to lose face, then I thought to myself I must be selfish.*

Therapist: *So do you believe a little child of two or three wanting her father's attention or making a bit of noise is being selfish?*

Client: *No, that is just natural behaviour that I was being forced to suppress.*

Therapist: *So do you now believe that you are selfish?*
Client: *I must be because I manipulate people.*

Therapist: *So where did I learn to believe that I believe that I manipulate people?*

Client: *At school. Excellence at school, especially in the sciences, was what my parents appreciated, so I studied and worked really hard, all those hours. I worked to make them appreciate me. I knew if I could get good marks and be top of the class they would love me. But even though I worked very hard, I never came higher than second.*

Therapist: *So by working very hard to try to get your parents' love, you were manipulating them, is that right?*

Client: *I've got to open my eyes, I feel so dizzy, I feel sick.*
Therapist: *Kioto, that is your resistance talking, are you ready to work through that to get to the information we need right now to help you?*

Client: *Yes, yes, yes, I was manipulating them to get their love.*

Therapist: *So that every child who works hard to gain her parents' approval is selfish and manipulative?*

Client: *Well no, not really. But I was.*

Therapist: *Children are born with the right to unconditional love. Their parents have a duty to love and cherish and nurture the child. Tell me, who is failing, who is being selfish when a child has to work and manipulate to get attention, never mind the love that is her right?*

There was silence from Kioto and a few tears.

Therapist: *Kioto it's not your fault*

The flood gates then opened and she was almost howling like an animal, repeatedly saying *"It's not my fault"*. After a minute of sobs and tears the session continued.

Therapist: *So do you believe that you are selfish and manipulate people?*

Client: *No! It really was not my fault, they were selfish, not me. Expecting so much from me but never giving me any respect, any love.*

Therapist: *If that mistaken selfish belief had a physical form what would it be?*

Client: *It wears a metal suit, like iron and it has a long spiky nose*

Therapist: *What would be needed to destroy that mistaken belief for ever?*

Client: *A big hammer then I can hit it over the head - BANG - and flatten it and completely destroy it. (At this point Kioto was carrying out the actions of swinging a heavy hammer over her head then crashing it down on to her lap, laughing and crying at the same time, bouncing around in the chair.) It is done.*

It is interesting to observe that we have invariably found that when a topic is being dealt with that has a strong degree of emotional content, particularly where there is a strong element of denial linked to it, a physical form of resistance will manifest itself, attempting to disrupt the proceedings. The dizziness as experienced by Kioto is an example of this.

20.9 Control case study

Gemma is a 34-year-old director of a small manufacturing company. She initially consulted us for problems with panic attacks which she was experiencing in a variety of situations. These had expanded to include signing cheques in front of others, standing in queues, pouring coffee for visitors, driving (she was no longer driving), being in trains or aeroplanes, being around strangers - in particular those in positions of power or authority.

Gemma was terrified of losing control and did not want to enter any altered states. It was her dislike of the idea of hypnosis which meant she was willing to consider using GOLD Counselling™ to alleviate her problem. This fear was so profound that she would not even sit in an inclined chair but instead always sat on a hard high-backed chair.

However, she was incredibly imaginative and was very capable at recall. Her first panic attack had occurred three years ago when she was asked to serve coffee to visitors - she had started to shake so badly that she had to get someone else in to make and distribute the coffees.

Gemma has a very abusive mother and an ineffectual father. The issue of control had repeatedly come up in earlier sessions so she was asked to complete a GOLD Counselling™ list on the topic of **"Control"**.

Topic: Control

A **Shaking, non-controllable**	F
B Not obeying, not assertive (work)	C
C **Bullying by my family**	E
D Passenger (car)	E
E **Anger**	C
F **Foolish**	A
G Training (on the job)	E
H Travel (train, aeroplane)	F
I Loss of control - vertigo	E
J Ian, America. His sister	C

Control

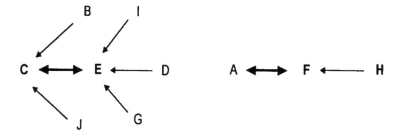

It can be seen that the Primary Belief structures were **A-F** and **C-E**.

Item J relates to Gemma's husband, Ian. He had been in America for a while where his sister lives. She had arranged a piece of work for him and was pressurising them both to move to America as she felt that Ian's work prospects would be enhanced there. Ian's sister apparently had a personality similar to Gemma's mother, one which is domineering and verbally abusive.

Because of her fears of losing control, the session was commenced by just asking her to close her eyes and to let her conscious mind be receptive to whatever was to drift up from her unconscious.

Therapist: *Where did I learn to believe the belief I am foolish?*

Client: *I feel foolish when I start shaking and then I get very angry at myself, my lack of assertiveness and knowing that I'm not in control.*

From this point, she digressed into explaining various incidents. Firstly that she had been bullied by her mother and brother. Then that her sister-in-law was trying to convince Ian to move to America when she did not want to give up her job and go there, and that she certainly did not want to live near this woman. Then that her mother had repeatedly told her that she "had nearly ripped my guts out being born", and lastly about all the things that she was annoyed with herself about. The final digression was of a memory of her father bringing strangers to the house one day who were dressed very similarly to the visitors at work at the time of her panic attack. Apparently Gemma had been about six at the time that her father brought those "men in suits" home.

Therapist: *So where did I learn to believe that I believe that I am not in control?*

Client: *It is something to do with those visitors of Dad's, they were important to him, to his business.*

After a great deal of exploration, and we were getting nowhere fast, we felt it was necessary to ask Gemma what had happened earlier in the day, before her father had brought his guests home.

Client: *We'd been up to London on the train, I'm not sure but I think my Gran was there as well. The tube was packed with football supporters, there was nowhere to sit and they were all so big. Someone gave Gran a seat but Mum and me were standing in the middle. They were all shouting and singing and then they started swaying, pushing from one end of the carriage to the other. I was hanging on to Mum and we couldn't do anything, we had to move with them. They were all so big and I couldn't stop shaking. I was getting squashed and I could hardly breathe and I was frightened I would fall and they would trample on me but they wouldn't stop. A man lifted me up over their heads and pushed me over to Gran and I was screaming and trying to hold on to Mum but she couldn't move, she was stuck in the middle and we couldn't get off because the carriage was so full. We had to stay on until they all got off and we missed our stop. I was so frightened I thought we were all going to die. Mum and Gran were trying not to show they were frightened but they were and I knew they were and that made me even more scared.*

All the time Gemma was speaking she was crying and shaking. Afterwards, she opened her eyes and said she now realised that this was where it came from. The following week she told us she had started driving again and served coffee without shaking at work (although she had been worried about this all day until the visitors arrived) but was still nervous about shopping and queues. Gemma had always gone shopping late at night when there would not be many people around and had always prepared the cheque prior to leaving the house. Her alcohol consumption had also dropped sharply during the week. She said she was feeling far more confident and in control than she had for years.

During a later session Gemma was taken through a list she had prepared on **"Queues"** and found that her limiting belief was about holding people up. Using the GOLD Counselling™ technique we arrived at a memory of how Dad had a thing about not being late or holding people up and used to get very angry with her if she was late in the mornings when he was taking her to school. He would deliver lectures about holding people up and how she was not important enough to keep people waiting.

The following week she came in almost dancing. That week she had been able to visit a major department store (previously a problem since she was required to pay on her charge card), gone on the lifts and escalators (previously impossible because of a fear of holding people up) and finished the day by buying petrol without a pre-signed cheque. All of this had taken place without any problems whatsoever.

At work there had been a group of important clients visiting. Gaining their contract could mean the difference between the company staying in business or folding. She had been a bit nervous for approximately 10 minutes prior to their arrival. Also she had been able to speak to her Managing Director about her always having to make the coffee because she was a woman. This had been bothering her for a long time but she had been too frightened to say anything.

20.10 Depression case study

This client had been suffering from recurring bouts of severe depression. The client was a woman of 27, married, with no children. Before working on "Depression," a map on "Anger" was prepared.

Topic: Anger

A	**Red**	E
B	**Crying**	D
C	Feeling let down	K
D	**Tears**	B
E	**Violence**	A
F	Shouting	R
G	Loud	H
H	Won't listen	E
I	Unfair	G
J	Hate	N
K	Helpless	L
L	Unpenetrable	H
M	Frightening	P
N	Wanting to hit out	R
O	Wanting to hurt	P
P	No control	N
Q	Feeling sick	R
R	Shaking	E

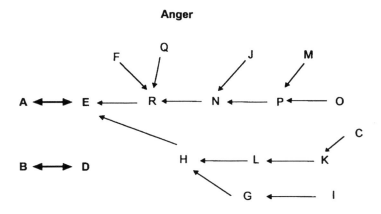

Anger

The GOLD Counselling™ list is structured around the Primary Beliefs **A-E** and **B-D.** The decision was taken to work on **"Violence"** and the session went as follows.

Therapist: *Where did I learn to believe the belief anger, violence? How did I learn to believe the belief anger, violence?*

The client found herself taken back to a childhood memory of violence between her parents. She was sitting on the stairs, seeing and hearing a violent argument. She can see her parents through a doorway. She was frightened just sitting there alone on the stairs. Their voices were loud, she felt their anger and she feels helpless. She didn't know where her brother was and felt totally helpless.

The adult client was then asked to imagine in her mind's eye going into the scene and rescuing the child. The adult took the child and stepped on to a cloud. The cloud floated up into a warm, blue, sunny sky. The adult hugged the child and told the child that she is safe and loved. The adult then told the child that anger was violence, back then, back there, in that scene between mother and father - now you can believe that you are safe, secure and loved.

Four days after this, a recurring bad dream that the client had been having about her brother, in which she felt anger towards him, stopped.

The client was then asked to prepare a list on **"Depression."**

Topic: Depression

A	Black	B
B	Dark	E
C	Despair	F
D	Guilt	N
E	**Hide**	**V**
F	Hopelessness	N
G	Worthless	O
H	**Weary**	**S**
I	Drowning	R
J	Lethargic	S
K	Confusion	R
L	Endless	N
M	**Blank**	**Q**
N	No control	P
O	Pathetic	U
P	Frustrated	K
Q	Dazed	M
R	Frightened	T
S	**Exhausted/weak**	**H**
T	Miserable	V
U	Tearful/emotional	T
V	**Shutting self off from outside world**	**E**
W	Avoid conflicts/questions	E

Depression

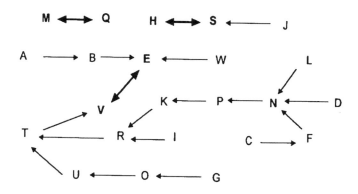

It was decided that we would work with **"Shutting self off from the outside world."**

Therapist: *Where did I learn to believe the belief depression, shutting self off from the outside world?*

Client: *I don't know.*

After a pause the procedure continued.

Therapist: *How did I learn to believe the belief depression, shutting self off from the outside world?*

Client: *I don't know.*

After a pause the procedure continued.

Therapist: *How did I learn to believe the belief depression, shutting self off from the outside world?*

ClientI don't know.

The client then recalled being a teenager and watching and listening to her parents arguing which then led to their fighting. She was distressed and left the family home and went to sit by the river. She had taken some pills with her. She was continually repeating, *"It's all my fault - I always get it wrong."*

Once she had arrived at the river she just sat there quietly thinking, feeling sadness and despair. She started to feel guilty about leaving her mother in the house and decided to return home.

She then remembered that her mother drinks and wanted to find a way of stopping her. She and her mother argued. Within the argument mother tells the client, *"It's all your fault"*, *"You take me for granted"* and *"I want to go away and leave you all to get on with it"*. The client felt that the situation was all her fault.

The client now focuses on the scene with her mother's drinking and feeling that it is all her fault that her mother drinks. The session then continued as follows:

Therapist: Who can stop drinking?

Client: Mother.

Therapist: Who can change drinking?

Client: Mother.

Therapist: Who owns drinking?

Client: Mother.

Therapist: Whose drinking problem is this?

Client: Mother.

Therapist: Who can change it?

Client: Mother.

The client was then asked *"What about me and how I feel?"*. The adult client, who is now feeling strong and confident, joins the client in the scene in her mind to explain to mother how she feels.

The adult client tells mother *"Drinking is your problem and you are the only one who can change it. It's not my fault"*. The confident client then takes the teenage client in her mind to a happy place where they feel safe. They have a hug and feel and know they are safe. They tell each other that Mum's problems are Mum's and that she owns them, both then and now, and that only Mum can deal with her own problems. The client then acknowledged that she is a caring and thoughtful person and can deal with and solve her own problems confidently.

Future-paced suggestions were then applied so that the client could carry out deep breathing exercises to feel relaxed and calm and to allow her to be able to deal with stressors in a relaxed, calm and confident manner. She was also guided to focus her attention on her breathing and find her calm place within herself whenever needed.

"Shutting self off from the world" occurred when the client escaped to the river to be alone. At the river the client felt *"Despair"* and considered taking her own life. She had felt that she had "No control" while watching her parents fighting. She had also felt *"Frustrated"*, *"Confused"* and *"Frightened"* while watching the scene. She had also felt *"Guilt"* about her mother's drinking problems.

The client was then asked to compile a list on **"Guilt"**.

Topic: Guilt

A	Letting people down	B
B	Causing people problems	L
C	Causing people/family worries	L
D	**Not being there for other people**	**M**
E	Not doing anything	O
F	Worried	J
G	**Tense**	**I**
H	Feeling sick	J
I	**Restlessness**	**G**
J	**Frightened**	**L**
K	Avoiding contact with other people	O
L	**Feeling people will give up on me**	**N**
M	**Unreliable**	**D**
N	**Unwanted**	**L**
O	Isolated	J

Guilt

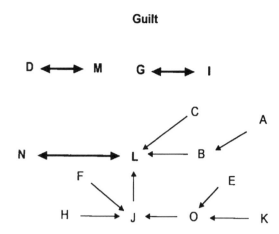

When she had finished she was then given the following guided suggestions. She was asked to imagine walking towards a door with a key in it.

Therapist: *Open the door and take the key with you. Step inside the room and
lock the door. Be sure that the door is securely locked and that
nobody can get in unless you choose to allow them. Turn round and
notice that the room is warm and welcoming. It is filled with pink
heart-shaped cushions. Go and sit down and get comfortable on the
cushions. Feel warm and safe and know that this is a safe place for
you to enter any time you want to feel warmth, love, safety, security
and peace. You can find this place in your mind any time you
choose.*

20.11 Relationships case study

The client was very anxious, nervous and totally lacking in self-esteem. He had sunk to an all-time low in his life. The first list on **"Relationships"** had confirmed what had already been discovered through other therapeutic interventions.

Topic: Relationships

A	Difficult	L
B	Hard	H
C	**Shouting**	M
D	**Fighting**	I
E	**Hate**	L
F	Hit	H
G	Busy	I
H	Sunday lunch	A
I	**Pain**	C
J	Love	E
K	Staying	B
L	**Mother**	D
M	**Unfair**	E

Relationships

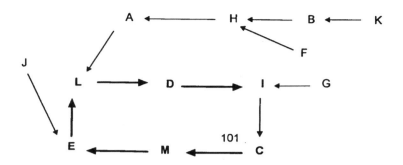

The Primary Belief structure for this client was **L-D-I-C-M-E**. Using this as a framework we worked with *"Mother"*, *"Hate"*, *"Sunday lunch"* and *"Unfair"*. It had been a shocking realisation to the client that he hated his mother for her unloving and critical attitude towards him all his life. Until coming into therapy he had believed that all parents had this attitude towards their children. The client also came to realise that his mother was incapable of loving anyone and not just himself. Also, after three failed marriages and a string of unhappy affairs the client had come to believe that relationships could only be hateful and unfair.

Through the work we did, the client came to understand where his beliefs on relationships were originally formed and, in fact, to whom those beliefs belonged. They were his mother's beliefs of how a relationship should be and not his own. The client also came to understand that our beliefs at an unconscious level will always fulfil themselves. Hence the importance of finding out where our beliefs were formed and by whom. Thus we have the opportunity to locate our beliefs and how they were formed and, where necessary, to change those beliefs by acknowledging to whom they truly belong.

While we do not usually suggest a follow-up list, in this case we were still working with the client and asked him to complete a second list on **"Relationships"** two weeks later.

Topic: Relationships

A Happy		H
B Strong		C
C Love		E
D Respect		G
E Joy		F
F Giving		H
G Sharing		E
H Caring		L
I Space		D
J Time		A
K Easy		C
L Flow		J

Relationships

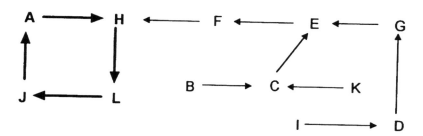

The fresh list revealed a Primary Belief structure of **A-H-L-J**. This is a significantly more liberating structure than previously.

20.12 Cancer case study

A woman client in her early 40s is experiencing cancer for the third time. The first occurrence was over 10 years ago, the second was four years ago and she is now undergoing chemotherapy for the third time. This woman originally came to discover ways of relaxing and reducing stress. Generally she had a poor self-image and was living in a very stressful environment. She is the mother of two children and presently the largest area of stress is being caused by not knowing if the cancer would reoccur.

Topic: Cancer

A	Scared	D
B	Guilt	C
C	Pain	P
D	Challenge	W
E	Panic	A
F	Helpless	L
G	Disbelief	S
H	Attention	V
I	Pity	P
J	Sad	P
K	Angry	V
L	Failure	R
M	Pressure	O
N	Change	W
O	Confused	N
P	Unfairness	G
Q	Isolation	E
R	Embarrassed	K
S	Shocked	E
T	Insecure	N
U	Unattractive	I
V	Negative	F
W	Positive	P

Cancer

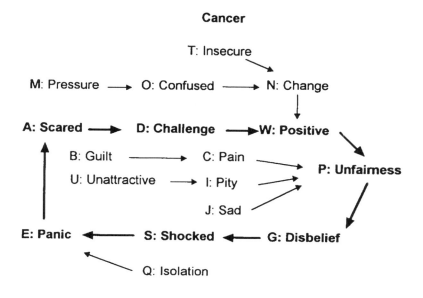

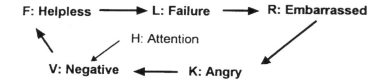

The point of weakness and the least anxiety-provoking item on the surface is **"Unfairness"**.

We had previously explained to the client, with some demonstrations, how beliefs are installed and also, at that time, she was taught how to relax her mind. We then asked the client the following question:

"Where did I learn to believe I believe cancer, unfairness?"

This question was repeated for about two minutes. The client then recalled that, at the age of approximately 10 years, her Mother was on the telephone talking to her best friend's Mother saying how unfair it is and is consoling her best friend's Mother at the loss of her daughter who has died of leukemia.

20.13 Eating disorders case study

This woman, was single, living with parents and her presenting problem was Bulimia. From a previous list of on the topic of **"I am"** a belief of **"Fat"** was extracted.

Topic: Fat

A	Ugly	GG
B	Huge	OO
C	Failure	T
D	**Mirror**	**RR**
E	**Uncomfortable**	**L**
F	Self-control	CC
G	Will-power	F
H	**Diet**	**I**
I	**Mum**	**H**
J	Sister	I
K	Stomach	L
L	**Bloated**	**E**
M	Nothing	MM
N	Thin	EE
O	Obsession	S
P	Attention	CC
Q	Ill	X
R	Worry	AA
S	**Constant**	**V**
T	**Food**	**W**

U	Disgraceful	JJ
V	**Always on my mind**	S
W	**Guilt**	T
X	Laxatives	N
Y	Sick	T
Z	**Panic**	**AA**
AA	**Weighing myself**	**Z**
BB	Scales	R
CC	**Achievement**	**DD**
DD	**Proud**	**CC**
EE	**Happier**	**FF**
FF	**Feel good about myself**	**EE**
GG	Hate myself	QQ
HH	Gross	OO
II	Pig	JJ
JJ	Compulsive eating	HH
KK	Calories	T
LL	Suffering	S
MM	Lonely	LL
NN	Bulges	PP
OO	Rolls of fat	QQ
PP	Hideous	OO
QQ	Pinching fat	C
RR	Always looking	D

Fat

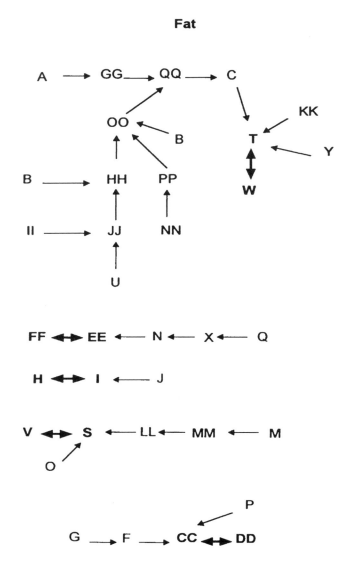

We asked the client to repeat the following question:

"Where did I learn to believe that I believe Fat - Mum?".

The client finds herself looking at Mum looking at herself in the mirror. The child identifies with Mum and feels that she is going to be like her fat. Her stomach is hanging out with rolls of fat, and the client is sickened by this. She doesn't want to be like her - it's disgusting. The client feels *"Panic"* (Z) at the possibility. The client then feels *"Guilty"* (W) at having these thoughts about her own mother.

Client: *"How could I think such a thing about my mother? I hate myself for thinking it." "I am alone in my bedroom - it's always on my mind thinking that I will turn out to be like her. I get on the scales and panic (Z)*

20.14 Learning difficulties case study

William is a very bright and active boy of twelve who is experiencing some difficulty with learning maths.

Topic: Learning

A English teacher		F
B English		A
C **Maths**		F
D Science		G
E Hard		B
F **Some is easy**		C
G Learning easy		J
H **Work**		I
I **Enjoy**		H
J Happy		K
K A's		M
L **1's**		M
M **Report**		L

Learning

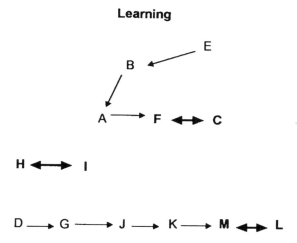

We decided to work with **"Learning is hard"**, because although the presenting problem was *"Maths"*, the words *"English"* and *"English teacher"* were listed as well and we felt that *"Hard"* would resolve the problem more quickly.

We asked William to repeat the question:

"Where did I learn to believe that I believe learning - hard?"

He recalled himself at the age of about seven years being sent to the headmistress' office because he had been naughty and written his name in a book. He didn't like her because she shouts. This headmistress teaches Maths and English and is telling William that *learning is the hardest thing he will ever have to do.*

Section Four:

How To Apply GOLD Counselling Techniques™ within NLP Procedures

Introduction to Section Four

Within Section Four of this book we have developed the connections between GOLD Counselling™and the techniques as incorporated within NLP. These connections are not meant to be exhaustive, and at our Counsellor's training workshops we would delve deeper into the full implications of the overlap. We feel, however, that for a competent therapist or practitioner it would be possible to quickly grasp the concepts documented herein and apply these ideas to your own practices. We have, therefore, briefly documented a suggested alternative approach for certain NLP techniques currently applied in therapeutic or training scenarios.

At the end of this section we have included a brief glossary of key words used within NLP. This is not meant to be an exhaustive list, it is purely to aid newcomers to NLP to understand some of the important terms within this field.

21. *How Gold Counselling™ Integrates With NLP*

As you will have now discovered, the beliefs which we hold control every-thing we say, do and think. It is only by operating at this level - that of beliefs - that we can create permanent and deep change for our clients. Within NLP there have been created many techniques and these can be grouped into different types. One quite simple, yet by no means exhaus-tive, categorisation is to recognise that some techniques focus on language patterns, others focus on pseudo-orientation in time and others focus on pseudo-orientation in space. All these techniques have the capacity to create significant change for people.

However, unless the therapist can determine the underlying beliefs which explain why a client is carrying out his problem state or habit, change will not be permanent. By taking your client through a GOLD Counselling™ analysis it is possible to identify exactly what it is that is holding him back from achieving what he desires. Once this is released, the tools and techniques developed within NLP can then be used, knowing that the original barriers to success have been removed.

Within NLP there exists the concepts of Metaprograms. (Dilts, R., 1990.) These are the sensory filters which we use to sift and sort information and thoughts. When your client generates his list of beliefs you will be presented with a detailed audit of exactly what Metaprograms he applies to his thoughts. This will enable you to understand further how and why his current problems exist and then how to "speak his language" when helping him.

By asking your client to complete a list of beliefs for a chosen topic you will also be able to work with him using the appropriate modalities for the different elements of his problem. Since he has written down the thoughts in his own words, the exact language to be used has been presented to you.

As you read the next chapters you will recognise how the approach as set out within GOLD Counselling™ will enable you to become even more successful at using NLP by focusing your skills precisely on the correct areas of your client's experiences.

22. *Eliminating Operator Influence*

One of the paradigms within NLP is that you cannot not influence, you can only not notice the influence that you have made. When using GOLD Counselling™ this restriction no longer applies. You are now able to not influence the client since the information he provides will be in his own language and from his own mind. This is so for the following reasons:

By asking him to develop a GOLD Counselling™ map on a subject of his own choice we have not influenced him.

In asking the client to generate his own list of beliefs using his own language (including predicates and sub-modalities), we have not influenced him.

By asking him to join the map together in a way that's right for him, we are again not influencing him.

And, lastly, by asking that he take his mind back to a specific and central memory within his own belief map, we have not influenced him, only focused him.

This difference in the way GOLD Counselling™ works when compared to other therapeutic interventions is extremely important since if you are influencing your client, either by accident or design, it may well mean that when working with your client you will unconsciously guide him in the directions which *you* deem appropriate. In consequence, if his symptom or problem is related to something which you find uncomfortable to deal with, you may well not dig as deep into the true underlying reasons for the problem compared to other, more preferred subjects.

23. Anchoring: Why It So Often Isn't Permanent

23.1 Overview

Most of us have had times when we felt we were on top form, when everything just seemed to be going along perfectly. It was as if we just couldn't put a foot wrong. Conversely, there are also those days when whatever we do seems to go wrong. We say the wrong thing, do the wrong thing, or even forget to do things and end up feeling bad. Those positive states are often grouped together under the heading of good luck or good fortune, whereas when the negative states occur, many people put them down to having got out of the wrong side of the bed, or one of those types of days, or just one of those things.

In the same way, there are positive states which we can seem to achieve, often without thinking about them, such as falling in love or relaxing when lying back on a soft bed at the end of a long, hard day. Imagine the sounds of popping champagne corks and glasses tinkling together and most people would associate these sounds and images with joyful feelings.

The technical term for the way that one's body goes into these different states is through anchoring. An anchor can be simply and easily described as *any stimulus which evokes a consistent response pattern from a person* (Grinder & Bandler, 1981).

23.2 How anchors develop automatically

Anchors are all around us. We all develop anchors from a very early age. Consider how a baby learns that when he cries, his mummy will pick him up and comfort him, (or rather, he hopes that she will). These early anchors which are formed are automatic and many of the other anchors which we develop are formed in this automatic, unconscious way as well. Habits, such as learning to walk, riding a bike, or even understanding these words on the page in front of you now are examples of complex anchors. In each case, once learnt they are consigned to the unconscious mind for it to administer and a very good job it does for us.

Problems arise as we grow up and we start to receive different and conflicting messages which have the effect of confusing us and reducing the clarity of our true feelings. Perhaps we have come from a background where we've only ever been praised for what we do, not who we are. Or perhaps we've been conditioned to get on and do things for ourselves and not to ask for help - even if we also feel that it's not weak, or not stupid, to ask for such help.

23.3 How we create anchors by choice

During our NLP training it is explained that through using anchoring we are able to first select a desired state, and then to anchor it so that we can reaccess this state at will. There are obviously hundreds of different states of desirable emotional feeling and, of those, some of the most frequently-suggested states which people wish to anchor are such things as:

a) happiness

b) calmness

c) relaxation

d) love or tenderness

e) motivation

23.4 Problems with anchoring

However, if we think back to one of the structural pre-suppositions of GOLD Counselling™, we must remember that it has been stated that:

To achieve a goal or feeling or objective, one must first remove the beliefs that are being fulfilled which are exactly 180° in the opposite direction. Rather than add positive thinking, first remove negative thinking.

If we take this concept a step further, let us, therefore, determine the opposite states to each of those listed above:

a) sadness

b) nervousness

c) tension

d) rejection or coldness

e) lethargy or apathy

What is normally found is that most people know exactly what the positive states are which they wish to anchor, but it is this second list of opposite and limiting states which keep on surfacing within their lives. Using the methodologies embodied within GOLD Counselling™ it is possible to identify and eliminate the exact root causes of these opposite states, so that the original desired state can then be accessed at will.

If it is true that people have all the resources which they need, then it is through this removal of the limiting anchors which hold us back that we will be able to access those desired states whenever we want. From this position we will then be able to develop additional new experiences which serve to reinforce us as the new person we have become.

23.5 Revised procedures

Within NLP one is taught how to elicit a state and then anchor the related feeling, either to an external cue, such as touching a hand, or an internal cue, such as imagining a particular scene.

We can then use the various anchoring techniques, such as chaining anchors or stacking anchors, in order to develop within the client an even more powerful set of resources. One particular type of technique which is taught within NLP is the means by which individual resourceful states are anchored to different fingers on each hand, permitting these to be accessed at will.

Once you have understood the effect that the underlying negative beliefs will continue to have on your mind while they are still there, it is possible to understand why many anchors, even when set supremely well, will fade in a short time.

However, once you have eliminated the negative beliefs associated with the opposite state to that which you want to anchor, anchoring the new, desired state will be that much more accessible.

Let us take the example of a client who had a problem with not being able to create enough wealth in his life. Specifically, he was not able to move towards money successfully, always finding reasons why something couldn't happen, or why a way of doing something couldn't work. He had spent much time using the techniques set out within personal development literature and specific NLP techniques but nothing seemed to stay in place for long. While this may have been due to his own approach, we decided to work with him using GOLD Counselling™. This revealed underlying beliefs about always being poor in his childhood, but, the belief was continuing to operate in the here and now and was eliminating any possibility of his creating wealth for himself or his family.

Once this set of limiting beliefs was released we then restructured the remaining positive elements and future-paced him towards the success he would have now and this had the effect of creating positive anchors in his mind to create the success which had once eluded him.

24. Circle Of Excellence

This is a very simple and clever technique which can be taught to clients so that they can very quickly and easily align their resourceful states by using a spatial anchor. If we again reconsider the presuppositions contained within Chapter 10, we should naturally assume that there could well be underlying negative beliefs which contain thoughts stopping them from automatically achieving their desired state.

By using the standard framework of the GOLD Counselling™language we can identify with the client when it was that he first learnt to believe that he was not able to access his desired state.

Let us use the example of a person who is having problems with a lack of confidence. If asked to be more specific he may say the most noticeable situation is one of staying confident while interacting with his superiors. Dealing with this may be a simple matter of revealing when he first felt unconfident when with his superiors.

It would then be appropriate to ask a question such as, *"What do you need to believe to believe that you can be confident in front of your superiors?"* This will cause his unconscious mind to imagine and access the desired state. At this stage, significant changework has already taken place. We could then enhance his confidence further by employing the Circle of Excellence technique, whereby we can identify and add other emotional states, perhaps taking examples of associated feelings he would find useful in his selected situation.

25. *Internal Conflict Manager*

As practitioners one can be presented with many different types of problems by clients. However, many of these can be chunked up to one of the following two formats:

1. *"Well, I'd really like to be able to do X, but then I feel Y and then just can't."*

or

2. *"Well, I want to stop doing X, but then something stops me."*

From both of these scenarios it is clear that there is some inner disagreement which is taking place within the client's unconscious mind. What we need to be able to do for our client in this situation is enable him to resolve this pulling in opposite directions and align the two (or more) elements for him.

From reference to the pre-suppositions of GOLD Counselling™ we would expect that there are two or more inappropriately matched and opposing beliefs at the centre of this problem. Following a brief questioning phase with the client, it would be possible to determine whether two separate topic lists need to be constructed, or whether a single map will cover all beliefs, including the opposing beliefs.

Once the GOLD Counselling™ topic list has been produced and worked through, additional work, such as the Internal Conflict Manager where the practitioner can guide the client to firstly separate out each part and secondly determine what the positive intentions are underlying each of these parts. From this position of understanding the practitioner can then have the client negotiate an agreement between all of these parts. This should result in these parts no longer causing the client to be pulled in different directions.

This approach relies on consensus between the parts, therefore all of the parts will still be in place when the technique is completed. Furthermore, any limitations put in place from any of the parts will impact upon and reduce the flexibility of the other parts.

What needs to happen is the practitioner can apply a technique which removes any of the parts that are found to be no longer be of use. Once this occurs, the remaining parts can be integrated in a strong, positive and congruent fashion.

could then be expertly applied to the precise memories which have been found to underpin the unconscious disagreement.

26. *Visual-Kinaesthetic Disassociation* (Fast Phobia Cure)

26.1 How phobias are created

As we go through life we are all presented with many different and varied situations. Some of these are pleasant, some are mediocre and some are distinctly unpalatable. Of those which are unpleasant, there are sometimes incidences which are so uncomfortable, so unpalatable that the person experiencing these becomes revolted by the incident. It is at this stage in the mental process that a phobia can become formed. This happens when the unconscious mind takes a single element from the original memory and then whenever this element is experienced, a phobic reaction occurs.

Take the example of a young boy who experiences being locked in a dark room. The incident would be repressed, but the emotional fear that the young boy felt would become attached to the idea of being alone in a dark room. Once this process has occurred the experience becomes lodged as a memory within his unconscious mind. Following this, whenever he is presented with a situation which resembles the original experience (i.e. has the element of the dark room), he suffers anxiety, nausea or fear.

It is an unfortunate fact that many people seem to develop phobias. Quite often people do not recognise that what they have always put down as their *"silly little foible"* is actually a phobic response to something. Our records show that there are over two hundred recognised phobias and probably many more as yet unnamed versions. In simple terms, there are as many different phobias as there are things to fear or situations to fear.

Many people with phobias have to suffer in silence, rearranging their lives to fit round their phobia, often having the problems with the phobia compounded by well-meaning individuals with their messages of such things as *"pull yourself together"* or *"it's only a little spider."* Other comments often proffered by clients include such things as, *"but you're a grown-up now"*, or *"that was so long ago"* or *"don't let that bother you"*.

26.2 How phobias grow in strength

The problem with phobias is embodied within one of the most powerful iron laws which is written into the very fabric of all branches of psychology and self-development:

The thing you fear most is the thing you attract.

However, it is an unfortunate fact of life that phobias if left alone do not go away. No. They grow, slowly and surely, debilitating the person with the phobia more and more as time goes on. This means that the person who fears spiders will soon have to start looking in the corners of rooms *just in case* there are any spiders.

To explain this further we shall use an example of someone who was trapped in a lift. After a while he might find that other small rooms may cause him discomfort. Later on he may find the phobia has spread so he does not want to enter office blocks which have lifts. If left untreated, the phobia will later spread to incorporate not wanting to enter buildings *just in case* he has to use the lift in them.

26.3 The pure NLP approach (Bandler, R.,1985)

One on the most used techniques within the NLP Practitioners' tool kit is that of the double-disassociation, or the Visual-Kinaesthetic disassociation. This can be used to remove phobias which have, until now stubbornly, resisted any attempts at eradication through desensitisation, positive thinking or plain denial.

However, by the time the client presents himself for help, the phobia may well have expanded and changed in many ways. This means that although he may feel he has a phobia towards X, in actual fact, the originating phobia may be Y, something so uncomfortable and from so long ago that he has chosen to forget it totally.

If one were to apply the Visual-Kinaesthetic disassociation towards the presenting problem, provided that the problem was the original object from which the phobic response was created, the technique could be permanently successful.

However, how would you as the therapist, or how would your client, know that it was the originating cause, especially where one considers that he may have "forgotten" where the original phobia came from? It is because of this substitution effect of the phobic response that the underlying phobia could well be missed.

26.4 The NLP/GOLD Counselling™ approach

Nevertheless, if a client were to present to you with a phobia and you were to ask him to prepare and work through a GOLD Counselling™ topic list with you, it would then be possible to determine exactly where the originating memory about the phobia was formed.

Placing information about the beliefs and thoughts related to the phobia is less stressful than having to re-experience all the times when it had been triggered. However, the information collated in this way is very powerful and enables the therapist to use his client's unconscious mind to direct him to the root cause of the problem. This is then worked on directly to eliminate any further incidences of the phobic reaction.

Very often the client will realise during the session that the reason why he had always thought he had his phobia was actually incorrect. Once this confusion is released and the real cause identified, the phobia reduces and dissipates thereafter.

Furthermore, once the phobia has been released the therapist can restructure the client's positive beliefs about the object or situation which produces the phobic response so that he would then be quite ambivalent about the subject.

27. Swish Pattern

The Swish Pattern technique was developed to assist people in stopping unwanted habits by asking their unconscious mind to develop new and more appropriate behaviours to replace them. (Bandler, R., 1985.) We have found that through introducing GOLD Counselling™ at an initial stage of the changework, before using the swish to revise behaviour, a deeper, more permanent change will occur.

This is explained by the fact that the GOLD Counselling™ analysis enables the client to actually understand, perhaps for the first time ever, where it was that he learnt to believe that his habit, (e.g. biting nails) was an appropriate way to behave.

We have all been cautioned, when preparing our client for the Swish Pattern, to ensure that he focuses on what he wants in a positive way as a new person, rather than what he doesn't want. For example, if someone's presenting problem were that he bites his nails, we would ask him what he would rather be able to experience. He may well say something such as being successful, having manicured nails and good-quality skin on his hands, or perhaps seeing his hands holding the steering wheel of a powerful motor car. While it would then be possible to carry out a Swish Pattern with this information, the change would not be permanent. This is because no attempt has been made to facilitate in the client the removal of the beliefs that are related to his habit of biting his finger-nails.

Even if we ask him why he does it, he will only be able to answer using his conscious awareness since if he really knew why he continues to bite his fingers, he would be able to exert his conscious will-power and cease the habit permanently.

What we must do is to generate a GOLD Counselling™ topic list whose subject matter will be the exact habit which is presented. This analysis will enable the therapist to determine when and where the habit was installed. Following its release, a new and appropriate behaviour can be integrated that will be lasting, since the client will no longer have any resistance to the new habit becoming permanent.

28. New Behaviour Generator Strategies

28.1 Creating new states

So many people, when first introduced to the New Behaviour Generation techniques are simply amazed by their powerful simplicity. (Dilts, R., Grinder, J., Bandler, R., Delozier, J., 1978.) Through this technique it is possible for new behaviours and new ways of thinking and acting to be quickly and accurately first modelled and then learned.

This element of NLP practitioner training can have a powerful effect on most participants' lives since it means that they can now generate in an instant new patterns of behaviour.

One of the key tenets of NLP is that all people already have within them all the resources which they need. Even if they have only ever been able to obtain that feeling, perhaps, of success or elation or calmness for just a few seconds, they have experienced it. They already know in both a psychological and a physiological way exactly what the experience is which they want.

So many people don't realise that they do have within them the resources which they need. However, we as therapists need to let them first understand that if they do want a particular state of mind, they must have been able to imagine it or else they wouldn't know whether they had really wanted it originally.

The challenge faced by those same people is that they are not able to, on a consistent and automatic basis, access those feelings which they feel they truly desire. For many varied reasons the same people are finding it difficult or perhaps impossible to access that particular state of emotion freely whenever they deem it appropriate.

28.2 Incorporation of GOLD™ Counselling

By including the GOLD Counselling™ approach at a preliminary stage of conducting sessions with the client, it is then possible to confirm where the limiting beliefs were first installed and then to remove them. Once this is completed, reinforcing beliefs can be added to ensure that the new behaviour becomes permanent. At this stage, utilising the New Behaviour Generator and specifically-worded suggestions, using GOLD Counselling™ language or the Milton Model, one can ensure that the client is now fully and concurrently aligned with the beliefs he now seeks.

Let us now use as an example a client who told us the following:

Client: *... and what I'd really like to do is just tell them what I think, but I don't feel able, or confident enough to do so. Yes. That's what I need, more confidence. Can you help me?*

In this instance we know that from within the framework of GOLD Counselling™ we would anticipate that one or more of these statements is true:

1. he really does not know how to do what he wants, which is unlikely since he does know what it is that he wants to be able to do

2. he doesn't really feel that he deserves to, should do, can do or such like, due to another, probably hidden, limiting belief

3. he has tried this desired state before, perhaps many times over many years, or perhaps just once, and the feelings associated with that failure were so powerful that further attempts have been precluded

4. his problem is actually a symptom of something else - his mind is letting him focus on this so as to guide him away from the real issue which is out of his conscious awareness

From a cognitive review of these permutations, it is possible to understand that if one were to adhere strictly to the standard New Behaviour Generator without clarifying what is stopping the client from accessing the desired emotions, the positive effect of the technique will soon dissipate. However, by accessing the unconscious mind's information as to the specific beliefs held about that emotional state, it is possible to remove the limitations which currently exist. Once this barrier is removed the client will be able to access his desired state. This could be enhanced further through the existing New Behaviour Generator techniques.

29. Well-Formed Outcomes

If you don't know where you're going, you will probably end up somewhere else.

The journey of a thousand miles begins with but a single step.

If you were to review the various books currently available which discuss success strategies, or motivation theories, or ways to create happiness, you would be able to identify one consistent theme. In addition, if you were to study any of the various schools of psychology, you would find that they all have one issue which they all seem to agree on.

People who are most able to achieve happiness, stay healthy, enjoy life and achieve those things which they really desire, are people who have worked out what they actually want from life.

It therefore follows that these same people have, by inference, also worked out what they don't want from life, such as poverty, sadness, depression or loneliness. Now it may be that they have just focused on what they want, or perhaps ignored what they don't want, but one thing is certain, they know what they desire.

If you were to take a survey of how most people focus on their goals you would find that most people are able to recite the many things which they don't want to happen in their lives but they will often have problems with identifying those things which they do want.

On the occasions when a client presents this problem to a therapist, usually the next steps, as suggested by NLP and other personal development training, is to work with the client to restate what he doesn't want into what he does want. From this position it is then possible to get the client to co-operate with you to develop a congruent well-formed outcome which will move him forward to his newly-desired state or goal. Where this procedural sequence fails is that it does not address the underlying reasons why the person has not achieved his goal in the here and now. Consider again the pre-suppositions of GOLD Counselling™ in Chapter 10. In this we state that the unconscious mind does not understand the difference between either the past tense and the current tense, or the current tense and the future tense. Therefore, even though you may have been able to develop a supremely well-formed outcome for your client and elicited all the desired states which he needs, you have not removed the original limiting belief which has meant that success has eluded him before now.

It is this original and still-operating limiting belief which will reduce or even eliminate his chances of success. What is unfortunate is that the client will not realise that his old beliefs are still in place and he may return for further assistance to refocus himself on his desired goals. However, by using all your usual NLP and personal development techniques, after incorporating a GOLD Counselling™ analysis to determine why he has not yet achieved his goals, his success will be that much more assured.

30. Six-Step Reframing

In the same way as it is possible to enhance your successes with the Swish Pattern, GOLD Counselling™ can also be used to increase the success of the traditional Six-Step Reframe. (Bandler, R. & Grinder, J., 1975)

If we take, for example, someone who wants to stop smoking. Using the Six-Step Reframe technique it is possible firstly to identify the positive intention behind his smoking habit and then to utilise his own unconscious mind to develop alternative strategies and new ways of behaving which will fulfil the same purpose. While this technique can and will generate new behaviours, the session can be less successful than it first appears. This is because the client will not realise that the presenting problem - that of not being able to stop smoking - is actually connected to another issue linked at an unconscious level.

We would now always direct our clients to complete a GOLD Counselling™ topic list on **"Smoking"** which would be worked through before carrying out the Six-Step Reframe. In these instances it is invariably the case that the Six-Step Reframe will either not be required, or will be applied to an entirely different area of that person's map of the world which is the real and underlying issue.

This means that the therapist can apply the appropriate techniques to the appropriate causes of the symptoms and not merely address the symptoms.

As an example, consider someone who wishes to increase his confidence when undertaking public speaking. If we question him further, he may explain that he gets a nervous feeling in his stomach, linked to an increase in perspiration immediately prior to standing up to speak. We ask him to connect with the part responsible for this feeling and by clarifying the positive intention behind this will generate information. However, unless the originating cause that gave rise to this positive intention is removed, it will continue to cause a problem for the client.

This is when the concept of symptom substitution can be experienced. We must assume that a client would not come to us unless he were unable to change his behaviour himself. Accordingly, we must also assume that there is something within him but out of his control and it is this which the Six-Step Reframe identifies.

If we use the analogy of a computer program it is possible to understand with even more clarity the problems of symptom substitution and the effects of "and therapy" when the therapist seeks only to add positive suggestions onto existing beliefs without first addressing the cause. Many of you will have heard of the computer programmer's phrase "garbage in, garbage out" or "GIGO".

However well written a program is, it takes time and energy for this to be run and for an output to be generated, even if it is inappropriate or incorrect. This inappropriate output will continue to be produced even though it is useless, since the program believes it is required.

These problem scenarios are often not able to be identified when the program is first written. Many programs are so complex and contain so many permutations that errors cannot be found until many years after the original programming was carried out. The original program has often been written in a code which is no longer understood and, therefore, cannot be rewritten. This means that a new program has then to be written, running after the first program, compensating for the error, causing additional energy to be expended.

This is the same as "and therapy" where the error is not corrected but covered over, meaning that other problems resulting from the initial error in the original program permeate into other areas. As a result, additional work around programs will be required to correct further errors when identified. Every one of these will take time and energy to be run, causing the system to run slower and slower by taking up more and more memory.

Taking this into a client situation, this means that he will fabricate more and more procedures, habits and ways of acting to cover up and mitigate the impact of his underlying problem, without ever uncovering where the errant learning had first been written into his life.

Over a period of years a client may unconsciously generate tens or hundreds of small work-around programs, each draining his energy. However, once the original programming has been rewritten, all of these additional programs can be deleted, releasing the associated energy for use in other areas of his life.

Provided we take our client through a GOLD Counselling™ session which focuses on the habit or problem presented by the client, we will be able to determine exactly where his limiting belief originated. This will ensure that we can rewrite the errant programming instead of adding new programs to cover-up the problem. This simplification of his life will free-up energy and enable him to succeed in a simpler and easier way.

31. Stepping-Up And Stepping-Down Exercises

31.1 Overview

If you were to ask someone to tell you what is really significantly important to him in his life, you might well receive a response such as to make more money, or to have a bigger house, or to be able to spend more time with his children. If you were to take this as a starting point, you could then ask him to imagine for a moment that he had already achieved this goal. Then ask from that position, what would having achieved this do for him?

Within most styles of personal development and therapy techniques, it is taught that the goals and objectives that we have are in turn connected to other goals and objectives. It therefore follows that by peeling back these layers one by one, the underlying reasons why your client really wants to achieve something can be revealed. This can be best expressed as the difference between *"ends"* and *"means"*. With this approach, the therapist enables the client to convert the *"ends"* (the activity or result that he wants) into a *"means"* (to let the client gain a deeper understanding of what having this would do for him).

31.2 Stepping-Up

Within NLP there exists a technique known as Chunking Up. (Dilts, R., 1990.) If we use a simple example, we can explain how the method would be applied. Let us assume that a client has come to see you as a therapist to gain assistance in being able to change his career. In this event, the therapist would use specifically-worded questions such as:

Therapist: *What do you want as an outcome? (ends)*

Client: *To be in a good job with a much better income than my present one. (ends)*

Therapist: *And if you achieved this outcome of being in a good job with a much better income than your present one (ends), what would that do for you? (means)*

Client: *I would then know that I can provide for my family. (ends)*

Therapist: *And if you achieved this outcome of knowing that you can provide for your family (ends), what would that do for you? (means)*

Client: *I would know that I was successful. (ends)*

Therapist: *And if you achieved this outcome of knowing that you were successful (ends), what would that do for you? (means)*

Client: *I would know that I had done good, that my life was good. (ends)*

This technique would normally be applied by repeating the steps above until the client reaches a spiritual level, which is usually the deepest most profound state which he can achieve. By recording each of these steps and then taking him back down from this deep state to the original ends from which it was developed, a deeper understanding and focusing on his goals will be generated.

31.3 Stepping-Down

In addition to this, a technique has been developed which focuses in the opposite direction on the client's barriers to success. This technique is called, naturally enough, Stepping-Down.

Once the outcome has been identified, the first question asked is *"What stops you?"* Having identified this, the therapist then asks the client *"What do you want instead?"* Again, once the limitation has been identified, the client is again asked *"What stops you?"* By taking this exercise forward, stepping down and then down again, it would be possible to understand the real and underlying reason for not achieving the original outcome.

If we were to now revisit the same presenting problem discussed earlier, let us compare how the Stepping Down process would work.

Therapist: *What do you want as an outcome? (ends)*

Client: *To be in a good job with a much better income than my present one. (ends)*

Therapist: *And what stops you? (limitations)*

Client: *I'm not sure what I want to do? (limitations)*

Therapist: *And what do you want instead? (ends)*

Client: *To know what I'm good at? (ends)*

Therapist: *And what stops you? (limitations)*

Client: *I'm afraid that I can't find anything better to do. (limitations)*

Therapist: *And what do you want instead? (ends)*

Client: *To find a better career (ends)*

31.4 Problems with these approaches

In this way the client will be directed by the therapist to investigate the inner reaches of his mind in order to ascertain the barriers to his success and then to determine what he would desire instead.

However, both of these techniques carry with them a specific and dangerous flaw in their logic. This flaw is based on the premise that one can use linear logic when dealing with the thought patterns within the unconscious mind. We have found however, that the unconscious mind uses non-logical logic, or fuzzy logic, when processing thoughts and beliefs. If we reconsider the original presenting problem for a moment we can understand this more easily.

Client: *I want to be in a good job with a much better income than my present one.*

If we ask a logical question, we will be given a logical answer. We will then find ourselves drawn away from the deeper, unconscious beliefs which are really impacting on his success. This will happen because the client will not be consciously aware of why he is not achieving his desired goals. The only way to understand this is to map out his unconscious thoughts which make up his beliefs in respect of the subject.

31.5 The GOLD Counselling™ approach

This information would be revealed simply and concisely if the client were asked to prepare a GOLD Counselling™ topic list such as:

My career

Rewards

Job satisfaction

From this we would be able to determine exactly where the limiting beliefs are which are stopping the client from achieving success in the present.

32. *Reduction In Learning Difficulties*

Some of the greatest advances in NLP have related to the techniques developed for use in assisting people with reading difficulties to overcome their problems. (Jacobson, S., 1981.) For many people who have been assisted by these techniques, the changes which have been effected have been amazing.

It has been shown that many children appear to have problems when first being taught to read, which, if not dealt with appropriately in time, will have become accepted as negative beliefs about their abilities.

Much work can be carried out in trying to help these children (or at a later stage adults) break through the barriers related to their specific learning difficulty. However, we have found that in many instances, the actual blockage to learning - the negative belief - was actually formed before the attempts to learn the particular subject (such as reading words) took place. It is as if these children had learnt to believe that they were not good, competent or successful at learning anything as a result of that earlier incidence. Furthermore, although they may have hidden away the pain of the originating cause, the trauma of the original experience is still hanging over their lives like a thick, black cloud and continuing to affect them in the present.

Using GOLD Counselling™ in conjunction with your existing NLP skills means that it is possible firstly to determine exactly when, where and how your client learnt to believe the belief that he can't read, or he doesn't get maths right, or he doesn't like reading out loud. Very often, the belief was formed in a situation, perhaps only indirectly related to the specific subject where the problem now exists. It will, however, have had a profound influence on your client. Once this limiting and negative belief has been removed it is then possible for the therapist to use the wide range of tools which he has to assist his client in becoming the person he desires to be. This will be helped by the fact that the client will now have access to so many more internal resources than before.

Often when a client states that he is, for example, dyslexic, we find that it is a very specific type of dyslexia. With one client, he was managing his own building company and was capable of understanding technical drawings and carrying out mathematical calculations, although he believed he couldn't read or write. The GOLD Counselling™ session revealed that this belief was specifically focused on words and not numbers. As a result of a sequence of GOLD Counselling™ sessions, he identified where the repressed discomfort related to learning to read was buried. Once released he had no further problems and was able to continue with the learning which had been abruptly stopped during childhood.

In the same way a client will often believe that he knows he has a learning difficulty whereas he has often actually taken in the beliefs of his teachers or parents. It may, in fact, have been the teachers or parents who really had the learning difficulties. This can be evident in situations whereby a client's parents have had to leave school and to earn a wage at an early age. This fact can often be unconsciously communicated to children in the message that they should, in turn, also go out to earn some money. Once the client can identify whose belief this really is, he can then determine whether he wishes to take on further education himself.

33. Sports Improvement

Significant improvements can be made to the sports successes of people when the approaches within NLP are applied to their problems. Future-pacing, Circle of Excellence and New Behaviour Generator are three techniques often used. However, we have found that when a person has identified in himself a limitation, we need to assist him in permanently removing this prior to offering any further help.

For example, a client wanted to build more muscle. Regular gym sessions were proving fruitless. A GOLD Counselling™ list was prepared on the topic "**Weight**". During the session which followed he identified that the top part of his body was, metaphorically, stuck in childhood and only the bottom half had grown up. In the session he identified that the feeling of his torso's being small was linked to an occasion when he had been held down on his bed during a traumatic incident with his parents. Furthermore, regular bullying in school had meant that he had learnt to believe that he always needed to be a good runner. Releasing these incidents from his mind enabled him to realise the reason why his exercise program had always been focused on lower body fitness. He was then able to revise this to that which was appropriate for him now.

In the same way, many apparent limitations in respect of sports achievement and success are often found to link back to other apparently unrelated incidences which have occurred in the client's life many years ago. By applying the GOLD Counselling™ approach it is possible to identify and remove this unconscious limitation.

34. Habit Elimination Routines

Many people develop different habits, addictions or routines, certain ways of doing things which - however hard they try - they just cannot stop. These include physical problems such as hair pulling, smoking or overeating but these could just as often be a habit of regularly experiencing a certain limiting feeling, such as guilt or sadness.

In exactly the same way as we know how to be happy from earlier reference experiences which have formed a belief that we can be happy, these various habits which a client develops will have been generated from earlier beliefs formed from earlier experiences.

As a therapist, you must be able to locate the originating reference memories which have formed the client's belief that his habit is an appropriate way to behave. Once this is identified and a new viewpoint formed, the habit will cease. Change is natural and flowing and it is only the unresolved originating cause which is holding back the client's flow forwards with change. It is important to understand that the unconscious mind never does anything without a reason. Therefore, however apparently debilitating or destructive your client's habit is, it exists for a reason and until that reason has been identified and the errant belief revised, the habit will continue.

If a therapist only corrects the habit in the present, the underlying reason will still exist and will seek to generate a fresh habit within the client. However, by applying GOLD Counselling™ techniques to the underlying presenting problem it is possible to identify and eradicate the desire within your client's unconscious mind to continue with this habitual pattern.

In addition to the specific questions set out within Chapter 15, which reveal how to identify where and when a belief was formed, there are other questions which are specific to determining where habits were first formed.

When did you learn it was appropriate to do (habit)?

What needs to happen for you to begin to believe that (habit) is inappropriate?

By correctly identifying where and when the belief about the habit was first formed, it will be possible to remove from your client the need to continue with this habit any longer.

With some habits, such as eating problems, the underlying issue may be one of poor self-image or a belief about lack of self-worth or underlying guilt. Once this has been revised, the original eating habit will no longer be required and will disappear. Additional NLP techniques can then be applied in order to assist the person to expedite change into the person he wants to become, building on his existing resources.

35. Thinking Strategies And Negotiation Strategies

If we put to one side for a moment the idea of past lives and future lives, most people agree on one issue - life is not a dress rehearsal, it's the real thing. If this is true, why then do so many people appear to meander aimlessly through their lives, hoping that things will go the way they want?

Furthermore, we feel that these people are not just wandering through life aimlessly; they are fulfilling their beliefs. Their life appears aimless because they hold a belief which states that they hope things will become better - but not for them. This means that as long as they can keep their faith (religion) they will have their dream fulfilled in another life.

Set yourself up for success, not failure. So many people aspire to achieve greatness in life, but so few realise anything but a small fraction of their goals in the whole of their lifetime.

If one can eliminate the negative beliefs which have been incorporated into the unconscious mind, those which drive our strategies for behaviour, we will be left with only one automatic choice and that is to succeed.

An often-used quote which succinctly expresses this goes as follows:

Most people never plan to fail; they fail to plan.

However, the pre-suppositions within GOLD Counselling™ show that this statement is actually FALSE. People do plan to fail, it's just that they don't realise it. By this we mean that no-one would do anything which is alien to his beliefs about how he should act or think. Therefore, if what he is doing is unsuccessful, his beliefs - specifically his beliefs about how he should interact with others - have been poorly learnt. Perhaps it may be that the strategies that were taught learned at school are still being applied in his office life. Or it may be that the way he treated his college friends is the way in which he now treats his husband or wife.

This happens because, once a belief is installed, it is consigned to the automatic processing capabilities of the unconscious mind. If we no longer know it's there, how would we know when we are using it? Furthermore, if we don't know we are operating via a limiting belief, why would we consider changing it for something with more flexibility?

Let us take as an example a client who visits you in order to improve his strategy for financial management. From the initial discussion with him you identify that he appears to apply poorly-thought-out strategies for investment, linked to poor selection criteria. He feels that his approaches are rather hit-and-miss and somewhat erratic. In addition, when he realises that he has made an error, he is reluctant to act on this knowledge thus exacerbating the final financial cost.

It would appear that he would benefit from learning a new strategy with which to make financial decisions. One option would be to show him how to generate in himself the appropriate states of mind, such as a **dreamer** to create ideas, then a **realist** to bring himself back down to earth, followed by a **critic** to analyse and look for errors in logic. This was first developed from modelling Walt Disney and has become known as the Disney Creative Strategy. (Dilts, R., 1994.)

By applying this he would then be able to control some of his more impulsive and frivolous urges. Furthermore, if he were to read up on other financially-successful people and learn their techniques, we may well expect his situation to improve for a while.

However, if we were to apply the concepts within GOLD Counselling™ to this presenting problem, we would approach our client's presenting problems quite differently. Starting with pre-suppositions as previously defined, we can assume that for some reason and on some level our client does not believe that he deserves financial success. Furthermore, we would also expect to uncover a contrasting belief which he holds, an opposite, but still held, belief that he does deserve financial success. So he will continue to try to fail and then to try and fail. This, in effect, means that without knowing it he is continuing to fulfil all the Primary Beliefs at the centre of his belief structure about financial success, good and bad, empowering and limiting.

If we were to assist this client, we would firstly confirm the appropriate topic for him to construct using GOLD Counselling™. This might be "**Wealth**", "**Money**", "**Income**", "**Prosperity**" or whatever you as the therapist deem appropriate, based on your analysis of the problem and having listened to the specific language patterns used by him to describe his problem. After this you would ask him to create a list of beliefs on this topic. Once these were connected together, the GOLD Counselling™ session would be able to highlight the specific and originating memories from which the disparate and opposite viewpoints came. Armed with this information, you could remove these limiting beliefs and then consider teaching the client new and useful strategies for wealth creation.

It is only at this stage in the process that your client would be able to integrate into his unconscious mind permanently the new learnings as to the way in which he could improve his financial situation, since from this moment on, the limiting beliefs have now been removed.

36. Reframing

No particular situation or experience has any meaning other than that which we give it. By changing the "frame" that one views the situation through, it is also possible to change the meaning associated with that situation. This happens because in order to live in the world on a day-to-day basis we need to integrate that which our senses are picking up in the here and now with the existing maps of the world which we have already created from our past.

It is from the reference point of these maps that we will experience the world. Some people may see the world as a friendly place and will have reference experiences to reinforce that belief, whereas others will resolutely believe the world to be a dog-eat-dog environment and, again, they will have had experiences to justify that view of the world. We can only see what we believe, everything else is either repressed from conscious awareness or subject to kryptomnesia.

We have all no doubt found that the different reframing techniques are very effective in shifting the understandings of both ourselves and our clients in situations whereby a strictly analytical conversational session would not. Furthermore, we have often found that one insightful reframe, delivered in the right place and at the right time can create significant change in a person.

But how do you know that the only filter, or frame, through which the person views the world, is the one he is offering to you then? Or how do you know that perhaps the view he feels he has is in itself part of a much bigger issue, encompassing many more issues?

What is really required is a methodology which enables the user to understand what the real issue is which underlies that presented by the client. This is especially important when you consider that the client won't know what the real issue is, since if he did he would not have the negative belief installed any more and the feelings associated would have been dissipated.

Furthermore, the language used by the client when discussing his problem contains many deeper and more significant meanings, ones which are generated by his unconscious mind. To attempt to identify and reframe each of these would require a significant amount of analytical time, even supposing that the appropriate language became apparent.

However, by asking your client to generate a topic list focused on the theme which keeps on causing him problems, it is possible to identify the deeper structure to which the originating cause relates. From this position one can restructure the actual beliefs which are creating the problem, rather than have to reframe the symptom which is appearing in his map of the world. (Conceptually, reimprinting is drawn from the work of Konrad Loranz and his development of the concept of "Imprinting".)

37. Neuro-Logical Levels

The unified field of NLP as developed by Robert Dilts enabled us to understand how we can interpret our internal information and how external relationships are sorted. Since this is a holistic model, it also acknowledges that one element (such as our capabilities) can be inter-twined with other levels (such as spiritual values) indicating our overall direction in life.

When working with someone to align his neuro-logical levels, he can often become aware of when, in a particular part of his life, he is living and fulfilling negative and harmful beliefs. It also follows that as a result of aligning his neuro-logical levels, he will be much more congruent and focused within the different areas of his life.

Due to the various influences on our lives, it is possible to have limiting and even harmful imbalances throughout the various levels. Consider someone who believes that he is a successful businessman, with confi-dence and ability to create wealth. If, however, he also held spiritual beliefs, such as "the ends justify the means" or "might is right", he may then believe it is appropriate to do whatever he feels is necessary to succeed, even if this is harmful to others or illegal. This information would be revealed within a GOLD Counselling™ session and it would be possible to identify when the original learning occurred. Once this belief is changed, a profound realignment would then take place.

By realigning the neuro-logical levels, it is possible to gain a deep align-ment and spiritual balancing. GOLD Counselling™ can successfully do this by identifying where disharmony in different levels exists and by providing the means to correct them.

If we look at each of the neuro-logical levels in turn, then it is possible to appreciate where such blockages could arise.

Gold Counselling™

1. Spiritual *"This is my future"*

2. Identity   *"I can't change the way I am"*

3. Beliefs & Values   *"No one cares anyhow"*

4. Capabilities   *"I can't do it"*

5. Behaviour   *"I must work hard"* or *"I have to help people"*

6. Environment   *"I don't deserve a good place to live in"*

By working through using a GOLD Counselling™ analysis on the blockages which are identified, your client will be able to integrate new learnings at a very deep and profound level and ensure that his alignment, once set, will be consistently adhered to, since the opposite beliefs have been removed.

In addition, as a result of this realignment, any negative influences which may attempt to dilute the new quality of his life will be seen for what it is, since the original blockages and blind spots have now been removed.

Glossary
&
Appendix

Glossary Of NLP Words And Phrases

We have incorporated herein a brief glossary of the specific words and phrases used and defined within NLP. This glossary is intended purely to familiarise therapists who have minimal knowledge of the language of NLP with the important elements of the subject. There are many other books available which go into further detail on each of these subjects.

Anchoring The process by which a stimulus from an internal or external source causes an automatic change in a person's state. Once set up, whenever the anchor is triggered the linked state will be set off in the person.

"And therapy" Any therapy which seeks not to correct the cause.

Associated When one is experiencing or re-experiencing something as if one were actually there. See *Disassociated*.

Auditory Sensory input related to the sense of hearing.

Calibrating Using sensory acuity (see, hear, feel) to notice specific changes in a persons external state. And to know when changes are occurring in their internal state.

Capability The ability to use a particular strategy to carry out an action or sequence of actions.

Chunking Altering one's perception of a situation or event by shifting up or down or sideways in logical levels. Stepping up occurs when one moves to a level higher than the actual event in order to gain a new understanding. Stepping down occurs when one delves deeper into the event which one is attempting to understand.

Conscious All that one is aware of, right now.

Deep structure The underlying linguistic structure which is out of the conscious awareness of the person speaking. This is subject to **distortion, deletion** and **generalisation** prior to any words actually being used to express the deep structure of meaning.

Deletion	The unconscious process whereby one excludes a portion of an experience or a remembered thought.
Dissociated	When one is watching oneself experiencing or re-experiencing something with a consequent loss of intensity of feeling.
Distortion	The unconscious process whereby a current or remembered event is changed to fit one's existing **model of the world.**
Eye accessing cues	The movements of one's eyes, in regular and identifiable directions which can indicate what sense one is using to process information. These senses will be either **Visual, Auditory, Kinaesthetic, Olfactory** or **Gustatory.**
First position	Being fully in oneself and experiencing everything from within. Two other **Perceptual Positions** exist - **Second Position** and **Third Position.**
Frame	An outline or body in which a **strategy** can be modelled and then taught to others.
Future pace	To consider, in the now, how an event could turn out in the future, comparing actually desired results with what appears to be likely to occur.
Generalisation	The unconscious process whereby a single event or a few events are taken to indicate how all similar events will result.
Gustatory	Sensory input or recall related to the sense of taste.
Internal representation	The way in which we all store our thoughts, using the combinations of the five senses.
Kinaesthetic	Sensory input or recall related to our feelings, emotions or touch receptors.
Leading	Smoothly and discreetly amending your behaviour so that your client follows.

Map of reality	The individual and personalised way of experiencing the world which someone has built up, based on how he has experienced or imagined reality in the past.
Meta model	A model of language and its associated structure which enables the user to identify the underlying meaning of verbal communication which has been **deleted, distorted** or **generalised**. This permits the **deep structure** of the words to be identified.
Milton model	A model of language, exactly the inverse of the **Meta Model,** consisting of artfully vague language structures which overcome the filtering mechanisms within the conscious mind.
Mirroring	Copying the subtle portions of another person's behaviour. See *Pacing* and *Leading*.
Modality	Is a term that references one of the five senses, visual, auditory, etc.
Model of the world	See *Map of reality.*
Modelling	A key NLP process whereby one can elicit the syntax of the ideas or thoughts someone has to achieve a goal. This can then be taught to others.
Neuro-linguistic programming	The study of the difference which makes the difference - how different people structure their experiences and achieve their outcomes.
Neuro-logical levels	A model which connects six levels of experience together - **Spiritual, Identity, Beliefs, Capability, Behaviour** and **Environment**.
Olfactory	Sensory input or recall related to the sense of smell.
Pacing	Staying in step with another person's behaviours. See *Leading* and *Mirroring*.
Parts	The individual sub-personalities within us, usually with conflicting ideas and behaviours.

Perceptual positions	Our understanding and appreciation of a situation can be from our own perspective **(First Position)** from the perspective of the other person **(Second Position)** or as an observer of the interaction **(Third Position)**.
Predicates	The words which people use to unconsciously indicate through which **representational system** they are processing information.
Pre-suppositions	Specific ways of understanding how we interact which must be assumed to be valid so that it is possible to interpret the underlying meanings of these interactions.
Rapport	The act of generating and continuing to have a relationship with someone else whereby the other person feels he is being understood at a deep level.
Reframing	Altering a person's understanding and interpretation of a statement by taking a specific element of that statement and revising it, creating an alternative and previously-unrecognised meaning.
Representational systems	The five different sensory-based organising systems within our minds - **Visual, Auditory, Kinaesthetic, Olfactory** and **Gustatory.**
Resources	A method which one can apply to create an outcome, including such things as physical resources, memories, techniques.
Resourceful state	When one is in a positive, liberating and useful state.
Second position	Understanding an experience from the other person's position. See *First Position* and *Third Position.*
Sensory feedback	The information received from another person through their analogy

State	How you are feeling or experiencing the world at present. The combination of all your internal and external sensations.
Stepping	See *Chunking.*
Strategy	The specific and repeatable sequence of steps used by someone to achieve a specific outcome.
Sub-modality	Finite distinctions that are applied to our representational systems which affect the way in which we experience and re-experience situations within our minds.
Third position	Experiencing the world from the position of an uninvolved observer. See *First Position* and *Second Position.*
Trance	A state of altered awareness in which one is inwardly focused and able to access memory and imagination at a deeper level than usual.
Unconscious	All that is not within your awareness, right now.
Values	The issues which are important to you.
Visual	Sensory input or recall related to the sense of vision.
Well-formedness criteria	A methodology by which one can design an outcome which is achievable and acceptable to oneself and one which can be confirmed when it has been achieved.

Appendix I:

A guide to further reading

We trust that after reading this book you will want to incorporate these techniques into the existing skills which you already have. We would suggest that these books will help you to achieve this.

Georges Philips & Lyn Buncher: *Understanding GOLD Counselling™: The Work Book* (Forthcoming)

Richard Bandler & John Grinder: *Frogs into Princes*
Real People Press, Utah, 1990. ISBN 187084503X

Joseph O'Conner & John Seymour: *Introducing NLP*
Thorsons Publishers, London, U.K., !993. ISBN 1855383446

Anthony Robbins: *Unlimited Power*
Fawcet Book Group, New York, USA, 1987. ISBN 0449902803

Napoleon Hill: *Think and Grow Rich*
Fawcett Book Group, New York, USA, 1996. ISBN 0449911462

Deepak Chopra: *The Way Of The Wizard*
Crown Publishing Group, New York, USA, 1996. ISBN 051770434X

Edward De Bono: *Conflicts: A Better Way to Resolve Them*
Penguin Books Ltd., Middlesex, U.K., 1990. ISBN 0140137777

Robert Dilts with Tim Hallbom & Suzi Smith: *Beliefs, Pathways to Health and Well Being*
Metamorphous Press, Oregon, USA, 1990. ISBN 1555520294

Appendix II

How to join the Association of
GOLD Counsellors ™

The GOLD Counsellors Association™ (GCA) was inaugurated to ensure that all practitioners trained in GOLD Counselling™ techniques are assured as competent coaches and tutors.   Only registered GOLD Counsellors™ who have undergone a full and rigorous training themselves are eligible to register as trainers.

Within our organisation we offer a selection of training options.   These cover all levels according to your current experience and your desired knowledge. Introductory one-day or weekend seminars have been developed so that people with no prior experience of GOLD Counselling™ are able to learn more about the GOLD Counselling™ techniques.

Further training exists for practising counsellors and therapists to integrate GOLD Counselling™ into their existing skills so that they can apply their skills to achieve even more success with their clients.   Finally, we also have an additional structured training programme for people who wish to go on to become trainers in the GOLD Counselling™ techniques. This training takes place in recognised colleges and universities throughout the United Kingdom and Europe.

Specific training courses have been developed and are run to enable people to take these skills into other arenas such as business and sales development, stress management and the like.

The techniques documented in this book are very powerful and, in consequence, within our organisation we ensure that only qualified and competently-trained individuals are awarded full counsellor or trainer status.

For further details of the full range of training programmes and training materials available, including tapes of our books and training material, please contact the address overleaf:

The Association of GOLD Counsellors ™
PO Box 115
London N12 9PS
Telephone No 0181 446 2210
Fax No 0181 446 2210
E-Mail Address Eclectic.Therapy@BTinternet.com

We look forward to hearing from you and discussing your successes. If you have any comments as to the ideas raised from this book, please feel free to contact us.

Bibliography

Andreas, C., & Andreas, S. (1989) *Heart of the Mind*, Moab, Utah: Real People Press.

Andreas, S., & Andreas, C. (1987) *Change Your Mind and Keep the Change*, Moab, Utah: Real People Press.

Andreas, S., & Faulkner, C. (1994) *NLP The New Technology of Achievement*, London: Brealey Publishing.

Bandler, R., (1985) *Using Your Brain for a Change*, Moab, Utah: Real People Press.

Bandler, R., & Grinder, J. (1975) *Frogs into Princes*, Moab, Utah: Real People Press.

Bandler, R., & Grinder, J. (1975) *Patterns of the Hypnotic Techniques of Milton H. Erickson, M.D.*, Cupertino, California: Meta Publications.

Bandler, R., & Grinder, J. (1975) *Reframing: Neuro-Linguistic Programming and the Transformation of Meaning*, Moab, Utah: Real People Press.

Bandler, R., & Grinder, J. (1975) *The Structure of Magic Vol. I*, Palo Alto: Science & Behavior Books Inc.

Cameron-Bandler, L., Gordon, D., & Lebeau, M., (1985) *The Emprint Method: A guide To Reproducing Competence*, Moab, Utah: Real People Press.

Dilts, R., (1990) *Changing Belief Systems with NLP*, Capitola, California: Meta Publications.

Dilts, R., (1994) *Strategies of Genius, Vol 1.*, Capitola, California: Meta Publications.

Dilts, R., Grinder, J., Bandler, R., & DeLozier J., (1978) *Neuro-Linguistic Programming: The Study of the Structure of Subjective Experience, Vol I*, Cupertino, California: Meta Publications.

Grinder, J. & Bandler, R., (1981) *Trance-formations: Neuro-Linguistic Programming and the Structure of Hypnosis*, Moab, Utah: Real People Press.

Hall, E.T., (1959) *The Silent Language*, New York: Doubleday and Co Ltd.

Jacobson, S., (1983) *Meta-cation*, Cupertino, California: Meta Publications.

Jung, C.G., (1969) *Jung Extracts: The Psychology of the Transference*, Boston, Massachusetts: Princeton University Press

Lankton, S., (1980) *Practical Magic: A Translation of Basic Neuro-Linguistic programming into Clinical Psychotherapy*, Cupertino, California: Meta Publications

Lewis, B., & Pucelik, F., (1990) *Magic of NLP Demystified: A Pragmatic Guide To Communication & Change*, Portland Oregon: Metamorphous Press

The Anglo-American Book Company Ltd
Crown Buildings,
Bancyfelin,
Carmarthen, SA33 5ND
Wales.
Telephone: 01267 211880 / 211886

We trust you enjoyed this title from our range of bestselling books for professional and general readership. All our authors are professionals of many years' experience, and all are highly respected in their own field. We choose our books with care for their content and character, and for the value of their contribution of both new and updated material to their particular field. Here is a complete list of our publications.

Figuring Out People
    by Bob G. Bodenhamer & L. Michael Hall   Paperback   £12.99

Gold Counselling: A Practical Psychology With NLP
    by Georges Philips   Paperback   £14.99

Grieve No More, Beloved: The Book Of Delight
    by Ormond McGill   Hardback   £9.99

Influencing With Integrity
    by Genie Z Laborde   Paperback   £12.50

Living Organisations: Beyond The Learning Organisation
    by Lex McKee   Hardback   £14.99

The New Encyclopedia Of Stage Hypnotism
    by Ormond McGill   Hardback   £29.99

The POWER Process: An NLP Approach To Writing
    by Sid Jacobson & Dixie Elise Hickman   Paperback   £12.99

Scripts & Strategies In Hypnotherapy
    by Roger P. Allen   Paperback   £19.99

Seeing The Unseen: A Past Life Revealed Through Hypnotic Regression
    by Ormond McGill   Paperback   £14.99

Solution States: A Course In Solving Problems In Business Using NLP
    by Sid Jacobson   Paperback   £12.99

The Spirit Of NLP: The Process, Meaning And Criteria For Mastering NLP
    by L. Michael Hall   Paperback   £12.99

Time-Lining: Patterns For Adventuring In "Time"
    by Bob G. Bodenhamer & L. Michael Hall   Paperback   £14.99